Irregular diapetalous corolla

Corolla like that of the *Violacae*

Papilionaceous (or similar) corolla

Flowers with Gamopetalous Corolla

Regular gamopetalous corolla

Bell-shaped corolla

Corolla with pronounced petaloidal lobes

Irregular gamopetalous corolla

Corolla with bilateral symmetry, ie divided into 2 parts, labiated or 4-lobed

Corolla with bilateral symmetry, the inferior lobe being different from the others

Position of the leaves on the plant

Rosette

Alternate

Opposed

Verticillate

Imbricated

Shape of leaves

Narrow leaf

Broad leaf

Single leaf with more or less incised margin or lobes

Single leaf indented almost to the centre in the shape of a fan

Composite leaf formed by variously-shaped folioles attached to the same axis

Light requirements

 In full sun

 In half shade

In full shade

Humidity requirements

Soil humidity

Meadows, grasslands

Steppes, stony pastures

Grounds covered in rubble or stones

Woodland

Pastures

Peatbogs and fens

Running or still waters

Gravelly shores and banks

Moraines, screes

Rocks and their fissures

Pedology

C	Basic or alkaline soils, calcareous
N	Neutral soils
S	Acid soils

Phenology

Roman figures: indicating the flowering month

| I | II | III | IV | V | VI | VII | VIII | IX | X | XI | XII |

Altitude limits   Plant height

From 0 to 4,200 m (13,800 ft) above sea level

Scales from 0 to 120 cm (4 ft) and from 0 to 12 m (40 ft)

Plant properties

Poisonous plant

Medicinal plant

Essence-producing plant

Mountain Flowers

a colour field guide

The Conways of
Copper Beech,
Maescelyn,
Brecon.

9th May 1984

Mountain Flowers
a colour field guide

S. Stefenelli

English translation by Lucia Wildt

DAVID & CHARLES

Newton Abbot   London

Cover illustration: *Trollius europaeus* Globe flower (*S. Stefenelli*)
Colour photographs: S. Stefenelli, except
                     plates 108, 118, 154, 157
                     (Jacques de Sloover)
Pictograms: S. Stefenelli

British Library Cataloguing in Publication Data

Stefenelli, S.
   Mountain flowers.
   1. Alpine flora
   I. Title   II. I fiori della montagna. *English*
   582.13'0914'3   QK937

ISBN 0–7153–8339–6

© Priuli et Verlucca editori 1977, 1982
   David & Charles (Publishers) Limited 1982

Filmset by Keyspools Ltd, Golborne, Lancs
Printed in Italy

CONTENTS

INTRODUCTION

It is the sheer beauty of mountain flowers that prompted me to write a book about them; a book that would generate an ever-increasing interest in, and love for, those little plants which can be found in the most varied mountain habitats, from woodland undergrowth to meadow pasture, among stones or in moraines by glaciers, or even within fissures beneath snowy caps.

Each year increasing numbers of walkers and holidaymakers visit the mountains; each year the flowers, however common or rare the species, run the risk of extinction due to indiscriminate and senseless gathering. And senseless it is, because in most cases these flowers—so beautiful in colour and shape—enthusiastically gathered at the beginning of a walk, wither within a few minutes of being picked and are discarded by the path-side.

What is often incredible is the environment in which a small plant manages to grow and produce its splendid, vividly coloured flowers. It often appears among rocks, in a small niche or in a fissure of a rocky face. Despite adverse conditions this tiny plant has managed to develop and survive and we should be encouraged to pause briefly and admire it in its natural environment. And yet, quite often, in the blinking of an eye and with utter irresponsibility, that tiny life is obliterated: the plant will no longer be able to produce again what is often its only flower, and with the flower will vanish its chances of seed and self-perpetuation. Along the path there may be hundreds of flowers similar to the one growing in the rocky face, but these are hardly ever considered: preference is given to the one found in an almost unimaginable spot, and by plucking it one denies others the pleasure of admiring one of nature's miracles. All this because so many people lack all respect for nature, probably because they lack all knowledge of its essence and value.

Hence this book. Many have already been written, but this one is different in that it aims to increase the reader's knowledge of plants and flowers by an easier and more spontaneous system of research rather than by the normal methods of botanical analysis and description. The beginner is guided through the various stages of identification of each plant: from observation of the colour of the flower in question through the use of 73 symbols referring to 17 different peculiarities, together with two scales, to the identification of the plant and its habitat. Thus it becomes easy and entertaining to distinguish the monocotyledons from the dicotyledons; the annuals from the biennials and the perennials; the plant's various forms; its underground organs; the different types and growing habits.

The number of symbols is necessarily limited; consequently, the description of the plant's characteristics as indicated by the symbols is approximate. Identification is made easier by the presence of the common name above each plate. The Latin names are given with their various synonyms; also given are the family names, the colour or colours the plant may assume, and its world-wide distribution. One is also told whether the plant is common or rare, and whether it is endemic, ie restricted to a specific area, itself the result of particular events and ages, and possibly morphologically altered from its original form during the course of time. An endemic plant is not necessarily a rare one; the phenomenon is often widespread within its own habitat or within its distinct geographical areas. Finally, information is given as to whether the plant is poisonous, medicinal or essence-producing, and which parts of the plant are used and what their properties are.

From what has been said so far, one can assume that many of the plants which form the so-called 'alpine flora' are widely distributed, often throughout the world. Can they still be called 'alpines' even though growing on mountains other than the Alps? By 'alpines' we mean all the plants which grow beyond the limits of arboreal vegetation, whatever the mountain range.

Over the ages, alpine flora has had a very eventful history, particularly as a consequence of glaciations. It has often been excluded from the peaks of its origin and compelled to exist at lower levels, sometimes as far away as the sea, or to 'emigrate' to other areas. As a result of these 'migrations' one can find on the Alps, for instance, plants which originated in distant regions, sometimes from the Mediterranean basin, or as far away as Asia (as in the case of the Edelweiss) and which have had to modify themselves and adapt. Glaciations are also the cause of the formation of many endemic species which have survived within certain microclimates, within oases formed by the movements of the glaciers, by winds, or by general changes of climate. All this, together with the continuing evolution of all living species, causes all vegetal forms to be constantly dynamic. Plants have been known to alter their habitat within living memory: new species can be found where others once lived and have long since gone.

All plants and animals are named and classified using terms which may be incomprehensible and difficult to pronounce. There is a very simple reason for this. In 1735 the greatest naturalist of all time, the well-known Swedish doctor Charles Linnaeus (1707–1778), wrote his *Systema Naturae* (seven volumes), and in it he introduced the concept of family, genus and species, and first used the double nomenclature in latin which is still in practice today.

His system is of enormous importance to scholars and naturalists throughout the world for, by adopting one official language (Latin) in order to identify and define plants and animals, anyone can understand exactly which species is being discussed.

Following Linnaeus, many other naturalists and botanists used the binomial nomenclature to classify plants according to divisions,

8

classes, orders, families, genera, species, varieties, etc. The binomial genus-species is followed by the name (often abbreviated) of the scientist who established it. This is the reason for the use of the two Latin names, followed by a person's name (or abbreviation), and sometimes by a date indicating the year in which that particular scientist studied the plant and gave it a name to distinguish it permanently from others.

TAXONOMY

Taxonomy (genus and species) is in accordance with Tutin, T. G., Heywood, V. H., Burgess, N. A., Valentine, D. H., Walters, S. M., Webb, D. A., *Flora Europaea*, Vol I (1964), Vol II (1968), Vol III (1972), Vol IV (1976), Cambridge University Press.

Where the plants do not appear in the above four volumes (eg monocotyledons) the taxonomy follows Binz, A. & Thommen, E., *Flore de la Suisse*, 3rd ed. Neuchatel (1966).

Synonyms are based on the following publications:
Fiori, A., *Nuova Flora Analitica d'Italia*, Vols I and II, Bologna (1969). Shown as (**F**).
Binz, A. & Thommen, E., *Flore de la Suisse*, 3rd ed., Neuchatel (1966). Shown as (**BT**).
Hess, H. E., Landolt, E. & Hirzel, R., *Flora der Schweiz und angrenzender Gebiete*, Vols I–III, Basel & Stuttgart (1967–72). Shown as (**HLH**).

Other synonyms are given without quoting the work they have been taken from and are indicated by (*).

HOW TO READ THE SYMBOLS

Type of plant

1–1. Plant belonging to the Gymnosperms: acicular leaves, often very long, or scale-shaped. Woody stalk, usually with resinous furrows; naked ovules; producing strobiles (cones), galls or berries.

1–2. Dicotyledons: plants producing an embryo with two cotyledons; leaves are net-veined, palm-veined, shield-veined, or veined in other patterns but never with parallel veins. Stems with more complex structure, the vascular system forming annual rings; also present is the cambium, a tissue which allows the diametral growth of the plant and the formation of woody tissues.

1–3. Monocotyledons: having an embryo with only one cotyledon; leaves with parallel veins running lengthwise; stems with relatively simple structure, as the vascular system, lacking the cambium, is haphazardly arranged over the whole of the thickness. Usually herbaceous plants.

Plant cycle

2–1. Annual plant: lasting only one season and completing its life cycle with the production of seeds.

2–2. Biennial plant: surviving for two consecutive years; during the first year it only develops its vegetative system, during the second it produces flowers and fruits with seeds, thus completing its biological cycle.

2–3. Perennial plant: surviving for longer than two years, although not always of a woody nature.

Kind of plant

3–1. Herbaceous: having the consistency of grass.

3–2. Sub-shrub: a plant whose stem is woody at the base and herbaceous in the upper parts.

3–3. Shrub or bush: a woody plant, branching out almost from ground level and reaching a height of 1–5m (3–16ft).

3–4. Tree: a woody plant of large dimensions, having a columnar trunk with woody ramifications forming the framework of the upper part.

Underground organs

4–A. Root

4–A.1. Tap root: elongated main root from which secondary roots radiate and in turn ramificate; it originates from the collar of the plant directly opposite the stem.

4–A.2. Fasciculate roots: a system of several thin roots, all similar, all originating from the collar.

4–A.3. Fleshy root: a more or less conical root, sometimes spherical, with a more or less distinguishable apex.

4–B. Modified underground stem

4–B.1. Bulb: a shortened underground stem, protected by foliar and fleshy, superimposed organs (cataphylls); fasciculate roots develop from its lower part. Several types exist, among which are the scaly bulbs (*Lilium*), tunicate bulbs (*Allium*), tuberous bulbs (*Crocus*), etc.

4–B.2. Tuber: a shortened and irregular underground stem, thick and globular, fleshy, provided on the outside with buds (eyes) and internally with reserve substances. It is connected with underground branches carrying the roots.

4–B.3. Rhizome: underground stem more or less horizontal, knotty and irregular. It differs from a root in that it is provided with buds from which grow secondary, above-ground stems. The roots grow from the underside of the knots.

Stem growth

5.1. Dwarf plant: acaulescent (without stem or *caulis*) in the shape of a rosette; also with a stem growing to a maximum of 30cm (1ft).

5–2. Cushion-like plant: having tiny, thick-set branches which form a thick conglomerate.

5–3. Spreading plant: having ramifications of various lengths spread out on the soil.

5–4. Stoloniferous plant: a plant with branches spreading on the soil and forming new roots which in turn produce new autonomous plants (including some spreading ones forming occasional roots).

5–5. Erect plant: a plant with one or more stems growing vertically from the roots. Usually taller than 30cm (1ft), bushy or arborescent.

5–6. Rambling plant: with stem(s) initially spreading on the soil before becoming erect.

5–7. Climbing plant: having a generally slender stem which grows by clinging to other plants or to various supports by means of tendrils or discs; also a plant the stem of which grows by twining itself around the support.

Plant sexuality

6–1. Hermaphrodite: a plant with bisexual flowers, ie with male organs (stamens) and female organs (pistils) growing on the same flower.

6–2. Monoecious plant: having male and female flowers growing separately on the same plant.

6–3. Dioecious plant: when the male flowers grow on one individual and the female flowers on another.

Inflorescence
(distribution of the flowers on the plant)

7–1. Single flower: plant with only one flower, or a single flower on each branch or stem.

7–2. Amentum: a generally drooping inflorescence with small sessile flowers densely set on the axis.

7–3. Spike: a usually erect inflorescence carrying sessile flowers along a central axis. The symbol also applies to inflorescences formed by composite spikes.

7–4. Raceme or cluster: inflorescence formed by an elongated stem supporting pedicillate flowers. The symbol includes simple and composite racemes in their various forms: resembling an umbel or a corymb, with ramificated branches, defined or undefined.

7–5. Scorpioid cyme: inflorescence with unilateral development. The symbol covers both simple and composite cymes.

7–6. Corymb: inflorescence formed by flowers with pedicils originating at various heights on the primary axis and all reaching more or less the same level. This symbol includes both simple and composite corymbs, defined or undefined.

7–7. Umbel: inflorescence formed by flowers with pedicils originating from the same point of the main axis and reaching more or less the same height. Both simple and composite inflorescences are covered by the symbol.

7–8. Flat capitulum: the inflorescence is limited to a flat or convex receptacle; the flowers are sessile or have short pedicils, either ligulate or tubulate, often arranged to look like a single flower.

7–9. Oblong capitulum: a globular, oblong or elongated inflorescence, with identical flowers, either sessile or with brief pedicils, closely set along the axis.

Shape of flowers

8–A. Special flowers

8–A.1. Bare flower: flowers having no petals and often no calix, as in many grasses and some trees.

8–A.2. Composite: inflorescence consisting of several flowers either similar (*Hieracium, Crepis*) or dissimilar (*Aster, Arnica*).
Note: this inflorescence is included with the symbols of flowers as beginners might mistake it for a real flower.

8–B. Flowers with dialypetalous corolla
(ie formed by several distinct petals, either regular or irregular)

8–Ba. Regular dialypetalous corolla:

8–Ba.1. Corolla with 4 petals or petaloidal sepals (*Cruciferae*).

8–Ba.2. Corolla with more than 4 petals, tepals or petaloidal sepals (*Rosaceae, Liliaceae, Amaryllidaceae*, etc).

8–Bb. Irregular dialypetalous corolla:

8–Bb.1. Corolla like that of the *Violaceae* (violets, pansies, etc).

8–Bb.2. Papilionaceous (or similar) corolla (*Lathyrus*).

8–C. Flowers with gamopetalous corolla
(The petals are welded at least at the base, thus forming a single organ with more or less marked lobes and regular or irregular corollae.)

8–Ca. Regular gamopetalous corolla:

8–Ca.1. Bell-shaped corolla (*Campanula*, etc).

8–Ca2. Corolla with pronounced petaloidal lobes (*Gentianella*, etc).

8–Cb. Irregular gamopetalous corolla:

8–Cb.1. Corolla with bilateral symmetry, ie divided into 2 parts, labiated or 4-lobed: dicotyledons (*Labiatae, Scrophulariaceae*, etc).

8–Cb.2. Corolla with bilateral symmetry, the inferior lobe (labellum) being different from the others: monocotyledons (*Orchidaceae*).

Position of the leaves on the plant

9–1. Rosette: leaves arranged at the base of the plant in variously-shaped rosettes from the centre of which grow one or more stems.

9–2. Alternate: leaves growing on the stem at different levels, never opposed.

9–3. Opposed: leaves growing in pairs on the same level and opposed.

9–4. Verticillate: more than two leaves growing at the same level around the stem or branch.

9–5. Imbricated: leaves growing over one another, in well-defined order, like roof tiles, covering one another at the edges.

Shape of leaves

10–1. Narrow leaf: acicular, linear, lanceolate, spatulate.

10–2. Broad leaf: ovate, obovate, ellyptical, round, cordiform, sagittate.

10–3. Single leaf with more or less incised margin or lobes: lobed, pinnatifid, laciniate.

10–4. Single leaf indented almost to the centre in the shape of a fan, or radially: palmate, etc.

10–5. Composite leaf formed by variously-shaped folioles attached to the same axis: trifoliolated, pinnate, bipinnate, etc.

15

Light requirements
(exposure, heliophilia, sciophilia)

11–1. In full sun.

11–2. In half shade.

11–3. In full shade.

Humidity requirements (hygrophilia)

12. Soil humidity: humid or cool soil. If this symbol is not coloured the plant in question is either xerophile or has no particular requirements.

Habitat

13–1. Meadows, grasslands.

13–2. Steppes, stony pastures.

13–3. Grounds covered in rubble or stones.

13–4. Woodland.

13–5. Pastures.

13–6. Peatbogs and fens.

13–7. Running or still waters.

13–8. Gravelly shores and banks.

13–9. Moraines, screes.

13–10. Rocks and their fissures.

Pedology (characteristics of the soil, pH)

14–1. Basic or alkaline soils, calcareous.

14–2. Neutral soils.

14–3. Acid soils, siliceous, rich in humus and peat.

Phenology (flowering period)

15. Roman figures: indicating the flowering month.

I	II	III	IV	V	VI	VII	VIII	IX	X	XI	XII

Altitude limits

16. Altitudes from 0–4,200m (13,800ft) above sea level: the minimum and maximum levels at which a plant can normally be found.

Plant height

17. Scales from 0–120cm (4ft) and from 0–12m (40ft): indicating the minimum and maximum height a given plant can reach. Heights above 12m (40ft; trees) are indicated separately in the text.

Plant properties

Poisonous plant

Medicinal plant

Essence-producing plant

HABITAT

Climatic conditions in mountainous areas vary greatly from the plains to the snow-covered summits, providing a wide variety of habitats and thus very many different species of mountain flowers. The rambler or climber will know how changeable the scenery can be in the course of a walk or climb. At the outset one encounters leafy forests which are shady and cool; then come the conifers—first firs, then spruces, pines and larches—replacing the beeches to form a tall, dark and heavily-scented forest; higher up, the forest opens up and the trees become sparse and stunted. Once the last sparse trees have been left behind, one encounters scrubland containing shrubs and rhododendrons. As the summit is approached, the grass cover becomes patchy and shorter; stretches of grass alternate with patches of stone, moraines alternate with the first patches of ice, followed finally by bare rock or glacier.

Together with its climate and flowers, each type of scenery characterises what is called a *vegetation zone*. Following the recognised classification system, the area of plains and hills at the foot of the mountains is the *colline zone* which occurs up to 550–1,200m (1,800–4,000ft). This is the domain of food crops such as corn and maize, of vines and of oak forests, and extends to the limit of vine culture. Above this is the *montane zone* with its meadows and beech groves which extends to the limit of deciduous woods at 800–1,700m (2,600–5,600ft). The *subalpine zone* is the almost exclusive domain of the conifer—firs, pines and larches—up to the limit of coniferous woods at 1,600–2,400m (5,200–7,900ft). The region of the mountain pine, followed by dwarf shrubs and alpine meadows up to 1,700–2,800m (5,600–9,200ft), is the *alpine zone*. The shrubs include Alders, and there are sub-shrubs such as Bearberry and Whortleberry. Finally, as the meadows become sparser and sparser, the *snow zone* is reached, above the climatic snow line, where in summer only a few lichens and mosses grow in the areas uncovered by snow. Against this background mountain flowers take their place.

Plate 1   The resinous forest covers the steep slopes of valleys between 1,700 and 2,200–2,400m (5,600 and 7,200–7,900ft). Some mountain flowers, such as the Twin-flower (pl 16), the One-flowered wintergreen (pl 14) or the Large speedwell (pl 86), will only grow in the shelter of this forest. Clearings interrupt the forest to make way for the meadows and pastures (towards the bottom of the plate). It is in these stretches of grass that the Globe flower (pl 32) flourishes, as well

19

as Arnica (pl 53), Purple gentian (pl 120), Mountain cornflower (pl 151) and many others. Higher up, the more rugged climatic conditions prevent trees from growing and the forest grows thinner and finally disappears. The natural boundary of the trees appears towards the top of the plate; it varies in altitude according to the exposure and the latitude of the mountain range.

Plate 2 At the foot of the slope of this valley the coniferous forest dies away on the steep banks of the rushing stream; here can be found Masterwort (pl 13), White butterbur (pl 24) and Alpine butterbur (pl 87). Beyond the stream the grass, which is scattered with stunted conifers, is nothing like that of the meadow—it is a peat-bog, one of the most fascinating environments both from the botanical and the aesthetic point of view. The origins of this habitat, which is less widespread than the others, are to be found in the slow accumulations over the centuries of the residues of bog plants which still continue to pile up and thus raise the level of the peat bog; numerous species can be found growing there, such as Grass of Parnassus (pl 11), Common cottongrass (pl 27), Birdseye primrose (pl 83) and Early marsh orchid (pl 129), mixed with mosses or—where the soil is acid—peat-moss.

Plate 3 A high alpine valley, like that which leads to the Lauson pass (3,296m, 10,800ft), provides yet further habitats for mountain flowers. At the bottom, at a height of about 1,700m (5,600ft), a grazing meadow is cut out of the coniferous forest.

The forest climbs the first broken buttresses of the rocky outcrops but, higher up, the scattered trees give way to the stony alpine meadows, home of the Alpine anemone (pl 4), Vitaliana (pl 51), Alpine lychis (pl 62), Least Primrose (pl 66), Black vanilla orchid (pl 130) and Trumpet gentian (pl 131). Then come the snow slopes which, with the moraines, climb to the *névé*. On the right, some black rocky escarpments jut out; their crevices may shelter Rough hawkweed (pl 8), Yellow wood-violet (pl 48) and Black speedwell (pl 146). The great white scar which mutilates the scenery to the right of the rushing stream is a former quarry of *lauzes*—thin slabs of rock used to cover roofs. Vegetation has not yet succeeded in recolonising the quarry although it has been disused for over twenty years.

Plate 4 Scree, rocky outcrops and short grass are the habitat of the most typical and attractive alpine flowers—delicate plants, in cushions or little tufts, like Alpine rock jasmine (pl 84), Purple saxifrage (pl 113), and Mt Cenis bellflower (pl 149). In the little valleys and depressions in high-altitude habitats (see centre of plate) the snow takes longest to thaw, and these areas contain a highly specialised vegetation with more lichens and mosses than plants with flowers. These plants of the snow zone, such as Sibbaldia (pl 44), Retuse-leaved saxifrage (pl 119) and Least willow (pl 156), have only a few weeks to flower between the thaw which comes late at this altitude and the autumn which arrives particularly early. Although much reduced in height, these plants are still perennials, and may live

4

for many years in constant development. Therefore each of their summers, very short and precarious, is used to produce leaves and flowers which have been developing since the preceding autumn and to prepare buds which will lie dormant all winter, sheltered from the heavy frosts by the thick mantle of snow.

PLATES

The species have been grouped together according to their dominant colour. For ease of reference, these colours are indicated at the edge of the page.

Cerastium uniflorum Clairv., 1811
Cerastium alpinum L. var. *uniflorum* (Thom.) Fiori (**F**)
Cerastium uniflorum Clairv. (**BT**) (**HLH**)

Family: Caryophyllaceae

Colour: white
Distribution: Alps,
Carpathians
Frequency: uncommon
(endemic)

Actaea spicata L., 1753
Actaea spicata L. (**F**) (**BT**) (**HLH**)

Family: Ranunculaceae

Colour: white
Distribution: Alps, Apennines; temperate, cold and mountain areas of the northern hemisphere
Frequency: uncommon
Properties: (*roots*) emetic, purgative, sudorific, anti-bronchitis; *external use:* odontalgic

Anemone baldensis L., 1767

Anemone baldensis Turra in L. (**F**)
Anemone baldensis Turra (**BT**) (**HLH**)

Family: Ranunculaceae

Colour: white, pinkish white
Distribution: Alps, Pyrenees, Croatia, Carpathians
Frequency: uncommon

Pulsatilla alpina (L.) Delarbre, 1800, subsp. ***alpina***

Anemone alpina L. var. *typica* (**F**)
Pulsatilla alpina (L.) Delarbre (**BT**)
Pulsatilla alpina (L.) Schrank (**HLH**)

Family: Ranunculaceae

Colour: white
Distribution: Alps,
Central Apennines,
Pyrenees, Balkans,
Carpathians, Caucasus
Frequency: common
Properties: (*flowers and leaves*) antispasmodic,
sedative

Ranunculus glacialis L., 1753

Ranunculus glacialis L. var. *typicus* (**F**)
Ranunculus glacialis L. (**BT**) (**HLH**)
Oxygraphis vulgaris Freyn (*)

Family: Ranunculaceae

Colour: white, pink,
purple, reddish brown
Distribution: Alps, Sierra
Nevada, Pyrenees,
Scandinavia, Iceland,
Spitzbergen, Carpathians,
Alaska, Kola peninsula
Frequency: common
Properties: (*whole flowering
plant*) febrifuge

Ranunculus pyrenaeus L., 1771, subsp. ***pyrenaeus***

Ranunculus pyrenaeus L. var. *typicus* (**F**)
Ranunculus pyrenaeus L. (**BT**) (**HLH**)

Family: Ranunculaceae

Colour: white
Distribution: Spain, Pyrenees, Alps, Corsica
Frequency: uncommon

Thlaspi alpinum Crantz. 1762
Thlaspi montanum L. var. *alpinum* (Crantz) Fiori (**F**)
Thlaspi alpinum Crantz (**BT**) (**HLH**)

Family: Cruciferae

Colour: white, yellowish
white
Distribution: Alps, Tuscan
Apennines
Frequency: uncommon
(endemic)

Saxifraga aspera L., 1753
Saxifraga bryoides L. var. *aspera* (L.) Fiori (**F**)
Saxifraga aspera L. (**BT**) (**HLH**)

Family: Saxifragaceae

Colour: white
Distribution: Alps, Apuan Alps, Tuscan Apennines, Pyrenees
Frequency: uncommon (endemic)

Saxifraga granulata L., 1753
Saxifraga granulata L. var. *typica* (**F**)
Saxifraga granulata L. (**BT**) (**HLH**)

Family: Saxifragaceae

Colour: white
Distribution: mainland
Italy, Elba, Sicily, Europe,
north-west Russia, north-
west Ukraine, north-west
Africa
Frequency: uncommon

Saxifraga cotyledon L., 1753
Saxifraga cotyledon L. (**F**) (**BT**) (**HLH**)

Family: Saxifragaceae

Colour: white
Distribution:
Piedmontese, Lombard and
Tyrolean Alps, Aosta
Valley, Pyrenees, Norway,
Lapland, Iceland,
Carpathians
Frequency: uncommon
(endemic)

Parnassia palustris L., 1753, subsp. ***palustris***
Parnassia palustris L. (**F**) (**BT**) (**HLH**)

Family: Parnassiaceae

Colour: white
Distribution: Alps,
northern and central
Apennines, Europe,
northern Africa (Atlas), Asia
from the 50° parallel to the
arctic coasts, Formosa,
Japan, North America
Frequency: common
Properties: (*whole plant*)
astringent, antidiarrhoeic,
antihaemorrhagic, diuretic

Astrantia major L., 1753, subsp. ***carinthiaca*** Arcangeli, 1882
Astrantia major L., var. *nigra* (Scop.) Fiori (**F**)
Astrantia major L. (**BT**) (**HLH**)

Family: Umbelliferae

Colour: white, whitish
pink, whitish green
Distribution: Alps, north-
west Spain
Frequency: uncommon
Properties: (*roots*)
purgative; (*flowering plant*)
diuretic

Peucedanum ostruthium (L.) Koch, 1824

Peucedanum ostruthium Koch var. *typica* (**F**)
Peucedanum ostruthium (L.) Koch (**BT**) (**HLH**)
Imperatoria ostruthium L. (*)

Family: Umbelliferae

Colour: white, pink
Distribution: Alps, northern Apennines, central and southern Europe, Baltic, Urals, Caucasus
Frequency: uncommon (endemic)
Properties: (*roots*) bitter-tonic, carminative, diaphoretic, expectorant (bronchial system); *external use:* chewed to relieve toothache and migraine; liqueur manufacture

Moneses uniflora (L.) A. Gray, 1848
Pirola uniflora L. (**F**)
Pyrola uniflora L. (**BT**) (**HLH**)

Family: Pyrolaceae

Colour: white
Distribution: Alps, central Apennines, Europe, Caucasus, Korea, North America
Frequency: rare
Properties: (*leaves*) astringent, diuretic

Viburnum lantana L., 1753
Viburnum Lantana L. (**F**) (**BT**) (**HLH**)

Family: Caprifoliaceae

Colour: white
Distribution: central and southern Europe, Czechoslovakia, Ukraine, Caucasus, north-west Africa (Atlas)
Frequency: common
Properties: (*leaves*) astringent; (*fruits*) antidiarrhoeic; to be used with caution

Linnaea borealis L., 1753
Linnaea borealis L. (**F**) (**BT**) (**HLH**)

Family: Caprifoliaceae

Colour: white, pinkish white, pink
Distribution: Alps, central and northern Europe, Carpathians, Caucasus, northern Asia, north America
Frequency: very rare (endemic)

Lonicera xylosteum L., 1753
Lonicera xylosteum L. (**F**) (**BT**) (**HLH**)

Family: Caprifoliaceae

Colour: white, yellowish white

Distribution: Alps, north and central Apennines, Sicily, Europe, Caucasus, Armenia, central and northern Asia

Frequency: common

Properties: astringent, emetico-cathartic, anti-gout, diuretic

Aster bellidiastrum (L.) Scop. 1769
Bellidiastrum michelii Cass. var. *typicum* (**F**)

Family: Compositae

Colour: white, pinkish
white, purplish white
Distribution: Alps, Apuan
Alps, northern and central
Apennines, Carpathians,
Balkans
Frequency: common

Erigeron uniflorus L., 1753
Erigeron alpinus L. var. *uniflorus* (L.) Fiori (**F**)
Erigeron uniflorus L. (**BT**) (**HLH**)

Family: Compositae

Colour: white, lilac, pink
Distribution: Alps, Apuan Alps, central Apennines, arctic Europe, Pyrenees, Balkans, Carpathians, Caucasus, Tibet, Urals, arctic Asia, Greenland, North America (Arctic)
Frequency: not common
Properties: (*flower heads*) antidiarrhoeic, anti-gout, antirheumatic, balsamic, diuretic

Leontopodium alpinum Cass., 1822

Leontopodium alpinum Cass. var. *typicum* (**F**)
Leontopodium alpinum Cass. (**BT**) (**HLH**)

Family: Compositae

Colour: white
Distribution: Alps,
northern Apennines,
Pyrenees, Carpathians,
Balkans, Croatia,
Himalayas, Mongolia,
Altais
Frequency: uncommon
Properties: (*leaves and
flowers*) astringent, bechic

Achillea erba-rotta All., 1773
subsp. ***ambigua*** (Heimerl) I.B.K. Richardson, 1976

Achillea herba-rota All. var. *ambigua* Heimerl (Vacc. & Wilcz.) Fiori (**F**)
Achillea Erba-rotta All. (**HLH**)

Family: Compositae

Colour: white
Distribution: Maritime Alps, Carpathians
Frequency: uncommon (endemic)
Properties: (*flower heads*) tonic, vermifuge, diaphoretic, febrifuge, emmenagogue

Achillea millefolium L., 1753

Achillea Millefolium L. var. *compacta* (Lam.) Fiori (**F**)
Achillea Millefolium L. (**BT**) (**HLH**)

Family: Compositae

Colour: white, yellowish white, pink, red, purplish red

Distribution: Alps, Apennines, Europe, central and western Asia, Siberia, North America (naturalised)

Frequency: very common

Properties: (*flower heads*) tonic, astringent, haemostatic, antihaemorrhagic, antispasmodic, bitter stimulant; used in the manufacture of liqueurs and sweets

Leucanthemopsis alpina (L.) Heywood, 1975

Chrysanthemum alpinum L. (**F**) (**BT**) (**HLH**)
Pyretrum alpinum (L.) Schrank (*)
Tanacetum alpinum (L.) Schultz Bip. (*)

Family: Compositae

Colour: white, pinkish white
Distribution: Alps, Pyrenees, Carpathians
Frequency: not common (endemic)

Petasites albus (L.) Gaertner, 1791
Petasites albus Gaertn. (**F**)
Petasites albus (L.) Gaertner (**BT**) (**HLH**)

Family: Compositae
Colour: white, yellowish white
Distribution: Alps, Apennines, Europe, central Russia, Balkans, Caucasus, Armenia, Altais
Frequency: common

Carlina acaulis L., 1753, subsp. ***acaulis***
Carlina acaulis L. var. *typica* (**F**)
Carlina acaulis L. (**BT**) (**HLH**)

Family: Compositae

Colour: white, purple, brownish purple
Distribution: Alps, Apennines, Europe (from Spain to Russia)
Frequency: common (endemic)
Properties: (*roots*) bitter stomachic, carminative, diaphoretic, antipyretic, diuretic; to be used with caution as it is an irritant

Stipa pennata L., 1753
Stipa pennata L. var. *mediterranea* Trin. & Rupr. (**F**)
Stipa gallica (Steven) Celak. (**HLH**)

Family: Graminaceae

Colour: white, yellowish white, silvery white

Distribution: Mediterranean basin, central Europe, western Asia, Siberia, Africa (Algeria)

Frequency: rare

Note: the feathery awns cause the seed to be transported by the wind in July–August

Eriophorum angustifolium Honckeny

Eriophorum polystachyum L., 1753, var. *angustifolium* (Roth, 1789) Fiori (**F**)
Eriophorum angustifolium Honckeny (**HLH**)

Family: Cyperaceae

Colour: white
Distribution: Apennines, Europe, Britain, Siberia, Caucasus, North America, Greenland, southern Africa
Frequency: common

Asphodelus albus Miller, 1768

Asphodelus ramosus L. var. *albus* (Mill.) Fiori (**F**)
Asphodelus albus Miller (**HLH**)

Family: Liliaceae

Colour: white, pinkish white, greenish white
Distribution: Alps, Apennines, Spain, Pyrenees, Hungary, Balkans
Frequency: uncommon
Property: (*tubercles*) emollient, expectorant

Paradisia liliastrum (L.) Bertol. 1839

Paradisia Liliastrum Bert. (**F**)
Paradisia Liliastrum (L.) Bert. (**HLH**)

Family: Liliaceae

Colour: white
Distribution: Alps,
northern and central
Apennines, Pyrenees
Frequency: rare

Allium ursinum L., 1753
Allium ursinum L. (**F**) (**HLH**)

Family: Liliaceae

Colour: white
Distribution: Britain,
Europe, Asia Minor,
Caucasus, Siberia, Ukraine,
Kamchatka (Russia)
Frequency: very common
Properties: (*whole plant*)
depurative, gastric
stimulant, antihelminthic,
hypotensive, diuretic,
antiseptic, antiputrefying,
rubefacient

Platanthera bifolia (L.) L.C.M. Richard, 1817

Platanthera bifolia Rich. var. *typica* (**F**)
Platanthera bifolia (L.) Rich. (**HLH**)
Orchis bifolia L. (*)

Family: Orchidaceae

Colour: white, greenish white
Distribution: Britain, Europe, Sicily, Sardinia, Asia Minor, Caucasus, Himalayas, north-west Africa
Frequency: uncommon

Trollius europaeus L., 1753

Trollius europaeus L. var. *typicus* (**F**)
Trollius europaeus L. (**BT**) (**HLH**)

Family: Ranunculaceae

Colour: yellow
Distribution: Alps,
northern and central
Apennines, Britain, Europe,
Carpathians, Caucasus,
arctic coasts of Russia
Frequency: very common
Properties: (*root*)
purgative; slightly poisonous

Caltha palustris L., 1753
Caltha palustris L. (**F**) (**BT**) (**HLH**)

Family: Ranunculaceae

Colour: deep yellow, golden yellow

Distribution: Alps, Apennines, Britain, Europe as far as the Arctic, Caucasus, Himalayas, Siberia, Japan, North America

Frequency: very common

Aconitum vulparia Reichenb., 1819

Aconitum lycoctonum L. (**F**) (**BT**)
Aconitum vulparia Rchb. (**HLH**)

Family: Ranunculaceae

Colour: yellow, greenish yellow
Distribution: Alps, Apennines, Europe, central Asia as far as Japan, northern Africa (Atlas)
Frequency: uncommon

Note: very poisonous

Ranunculus montanus Willd. 1800

Ranunculus montanus W. (**F**)
Ranunculus montanus Willd. (**BT**) (**HLH**)
Ranunculus geranifolius Pourret (*)

Family: Ranunculaceae

Colour: yellow
Distribution: Alps, northern and central Apennines, Jura, Black Forest
Frequency: common (endemic)

Erysimum helveticum (Jacq.) DC. in Lam. & DC., 1805
(incl. ***Erysimum pumilum*** auct.)

Erysimum hieracifolium L. var. *pumilum* (DC.) Fiori (**F**)
Erysimum pumilum Gaudin (**HLH**)

Family: Cruciferae

Colour: yellow
Distribution: Maritime
Alps, Carinthia, Pyrenees,
Balkans
Frequency: rare (endemic)

Sedum acre L., 1753
Sedum sexangulare L. var. *acre* (L.) Fiori (**F**)
Sedum acre L. (**BT**) (**HLH**)

Family: Crassulaceae

Colour: yellow
Distribution: Apennines, Sicily, Elba, Britain, Europe, northern Asia, Asia Minor, northern Africa, North America.
Frequency: common
Properties: (*aerial parts*) diuretic, hypotensive, anti-arteriosclerotic

Saxifraga bryoides L., 1753

Saxifraga bryoides L. var. *typica* (**F**)
Saxifraga aspera L. ssp. *bryoides* (L.) Gaudin (**F**)
Saxifraga bryoides L. (**HLH**)

Family: Saxifragaceae

Colour: pale yellow, whitish
Distribution: Alps, Pyrenees, Carpathians, Balkans
Frequency: uncommon (endemic)

Aruncus dioicus (Walter) Fernald, 1939

Spiraea Aruncus L. (**F**)
Aruncus dioecus (Walter) Fernald (**BT**)
Aruncus silvester Kosteletzky (**HLH**)
Aruncus vulgaris Rafin (*)

Family: Rosaceae

Colour: whitish yellow, yellow, white
Distribution: Alps, north and central Apennines, Pyrenees, Vosges, Caucasus, Balkans, Himalayas, China, Japan, northern Siberia, North America
Frequency: common

Note: used in the tanning of hides

Geum reptans L., 1753

Geum reptans L., (**F**) (**HLH**)
Sieversia reptans (L.) R. Br. (**BT**)
Parageum reptans (L.) Kral (*)

Family: Rosaceae

Colour: yellow
Distribution: Alps,
Carpathians, Balkans
Frequency: rare (endemic)
Properties: (*leaves*)
astringent, vulnerary

Geum montanum L., 1753

Geum montanum L. (**F**) (**HLH**)
Sieversia montana (L.) R. Br. (**BT**)
Parageum montanum (L.) Hara (*)

Family: Rosaceae

Colour: yellow
Distribution: Alps, Apuan Alps, Tuscan Apennines, Pyrenees, Balkans, Carpathians, Corsica
Frequency: common (endemic)
Properties: (*roots*) bitter tonic, digestive, astringent

Potentilla anserina L., 1753
Potentilla anserina L. (**F**) (**BT**)
Potentilla anserina L. (**HLH**)

Family: Rosaceae

Colour: yellow
Distribution: Britain, Italy (Alps and central regions), Europe, Asia, North America, New Zealand, Tasmania, southern Australia
Frequency: uncommon
Properties: (*rhizome*) antidiarrhoeic, astringent, haemostatic, gastric tonic

Potentilla crantzii (Crantz) G. Beck ex Fritsch, 1897

Potentilla verna L. var. *Crantzii* (G. Beck) Fiori (**F**)
Potentilla Crantzii (Crantz) Beck (**BT**) (**HLH**)
Potentilla villosa Zimmeter (*)
Potentilla alpestris Haller fil. (*)
Potentilla salisburgensis Haenke (*)

Family: Rosaceae

Colour: yellow
Distribution: Alps, north and central Apennines, Britain (up to 1,100m [3,600ft]), Europe, western and northern Asia, North America, Greenland
Frequency: common

Sibbaldia procumbens L., 1753
Potentilla sibbaldi Hall. f. (**F**)
Sibbaldia procumbens L. (**BT**) (**HLH**)

Family: Rosaceae

Colour: yellow, greenish yellow, pale yellow
Distribution: Alps, central Apennines, Britain (to 1,300m), Europe, central and northern Asia, North America
Frequency: uncommon

Lotus corniculatus L., 1753

Lotus corniculatus L. var. *arvensis* (Pers) Fiori (**F**)
Lotus corniculatus L. (**BT**) (**HLH**)

Family: Leguminosae

Colour: yellow
Distribution: throughout
Europe, central and
northern Asia, north Africa
(Ethiopia), Japan, Australia
Frequency: very common
Properties: (*flowers*)
tranquillizer of the nervous,
psychic and cardiac systems,
antispasmodic, anticolitic

Tetragonolobus maritimus (L.) Roth, 1788

Lotus maritimus L. var. *siliquosus* (L.) Fiori (**F**)
Tetragonolobus maritimus (L.) Roth (**BT**)
Tetragonolobus siliquosus (L.) Roth (**HLH**)
Lotus siliquosus L. (*)

Family: Leguminosae

Colour: pale yellow,
sulphur yellow
Distribution: central and
southern Europe, Caucasus,
Asia Minor, north-west
Africa
Frequency: rare

Hippocrepis comosa L., 1753
Hippocrepis comosa L. var. *typica* (**F**)
Hippocrepis comosa L. (**BT**) (**HLH**)

Family: Leguminosae

Colour: yellow
Distribution: central and southern Europe, Bulgaria
Frequency: common

Viola biflora L., 1753
Viola biflora L. (**F**) (**BT**) (**HLH**)

Family: Violaceae

Colour: yellow
Distribution: Alps, Apuan Alps, northern Apennines, Europe, Caucasus, northern Asia, Himalayas, China, Japan, North America
Frequency: common
Properties: (*roots*) emetic, purgative; (*leaves and flowers*) depurative (blood), antiscrofulous, diaphoretic, bechic, expectorant, diuretic, laxative, emollient

Primula vulgaris Hudson, 1762

Primula acaulis Hill (**F**)
Primula vulgaris Hudson (**BT**)
Primula vulgaris L. em. Hudson (**HLH**)

Family: Primulaceae

Colour: pale sulphur
yellow, pale yellow
Distribution: central and
southern Europe including
Britain, Carpathians,
Crimea, Ukraine, Algeria,
Asia Minor, Caucasus
Frequency: very common

Primula auricula L., 1753

Primula Auricula L. var. *Balbisii* (Lehm.) Fiori (**F**)
Primula Auricula L. (**BT**) (**HLH**)
Primula ciliata Moretti (*)

Family: Primulaceae

Colour: yellow, sulphur yellow
Distribution: Alps, northern and central Apennines, Carpathians
Frequency: rare (endemic)

Vitaliana primuliflora Bertol. 1835
subsp. ***canescens*** O. Schwarz, 1963

Douglasia Vitaliana Pax (**F**)
Douglasia Vitaliana (L.) Pax (**BT**)
Androsace Vitaliana (L.)
Lap. (**HLH**)
Gregoria Vitaliana (L.)
Duby (*)
Aretia Vitaliana Murray
(*)

Family: Primulaceae

Colour: yellow
Distribution: Alps, central
Apennines (Abruzzo),
Pyrenees
Frequency: rare

Gentiana lutea L., 1753
Gentiana lutea L. (**F**) (**BT**) (**HLH**)

Family: Gentianaceae

Colour: yellow
Distribution: Alps,
Apennines, Sardinia, Spain,
Balkans, Carpathians
Frequency: common
(endemic)
Properties: (*roots*)
antifermentative, aperitive,
bitter digestive tonic,
febrifuge, vermifuge.

Arnica montana L., 1753

Arnica montana L. var. *typica* (**F**)
Arnica montana L. (**BT**) (**HLH**)

Family: Compositae

Colour: yellow, orangey yellow

Distribution: Alps, northern Apennines, Britain, Europe, Carpathians

Frequency: common (endemic)

Properties: (*rhizome*) rubefacient; (*flowers*) antiseptic, tonic, digestive, stimulant of the nervous and cardiovascular systems, hypertensive, haemosolvent, febrifuge, sudorific; must be used with great caution as it is poisonous

Doronicum grandiflorum Lam., 1786

Doronicum scorpioides Lam. var. *grandiflorum* (Lam.) Fiori (**F**)
Doronicum grandiflorum Lam. (**BT**) (**HLH**)
Arnica scorpioides Jacq. (*)

Family: Compositae

Colour: yellow
Distribution: Alps,
Pyrenees, Balkans
Frequency: uncommon
(endemic)

Senecio doronicum (L.) L., 1759

Senecio Doronicum L. var. *glabratus* Heg. & Heere (**F**)
Senecio Doronicum L. (**BT**) (**HLH**)

Family: Compositae

Colour: yellow, golden yellow, orangey yellow
Distribution: Alps, northern and central Apennines, central and southern Europe, Balkans, Carpathians
Frequency: common (endemic)

Cirsium spinosissimum (L.) Scop., 1769

Cirsium spinosissimum Scop. var. *typicum* (**F**)
Cirsium spinosissimum (L.) Scop. (**BT**) (**HLH**)

Family: Compositae

Colour: yellow, whitish yellow
Distribution: Alps, Carpathians
Frequency: common (endemic)

Tolpis staticifolia (All.) Schultz Bip., 1861
Hieracium staticifolium All. (**F**) (**BT**) (**HLH**)

Family: Compositae

Colour: yellow, sulphur yellow
Distribution: Alps, Jura, Balkans, eastern Carpathians, Albania
Frequency: common (endemic)

Tragopogon pratensis L., 1753
Tragopogon pratensis L. (**F**) (**BT**) (**HLH**)

Family: Compositae

Colour: yellow, pale yellow
Distribution: Britain, central and southern Europe, southern Russia, Caucasus, western Iran, Siberia, North America (naturalised)
Frequency: uncommon
Properties: (*roots*) edible, aperitive, sudorific, depurative, astringent

Hieracium peleterianum Merat, 1812
Hieracium Pilosella L. var. *Peleterianum* (Mérat) Fiori (**F**)
Hieracium Peleterianum Mérat (**BT**) (**HLH**)

Family: Compositae

Colour: yellow
Distribution: western and
central Alps, western Europe
to Lapland, Baltic
Frequency: uncommon

Hieracium murorum L., 1753
Hieracium murorum L. (**F**) (**BT**) (**HLH**)
Hieracium silvaticum Zahn (*)

Family: Compositae

Colour: yellow
Distribution: central and
southern Europe, Iceland,
western Asia, Siberia
Frequency: very common

Gagea fistulosa (Ram. ex DC.), Ker-Gawler, 1816

Gagea fistulosa Ker-Gawl. (**F**)
Gagea fistulosa (Ram.) Ker-Gawl. (**HLH**)
Gagea Liottardi R. & S. (*)

Family: Liliaceae

Colour: yellow
Distribution: Alps,
Apennines, Sicily, Pyrenees,
Carpathians, Balkans,
Crimea
Frequency: common

Lychnis alpina L., 1753

Lychnis alpina L. (**F**)
Viscaria alpina (L.) G. Don fil. (**BT**)
Silene liponeura Neumayr (**HLH**)

Family: Caryophyllaceae

Colour: red, purple, pinkish red

Distribution: Alps, Tuscan Apennines, Pyrenees, Scotland, Scandinavia, Iceland, Greenland, north-eastern America, northern Asia.

Frequency: rare

Paeonia officinalis L., 1753, subsp. *officinalis*

Paeonia officinalis L. var. *foeminea* L. (**F**)
Paeonia officinalis L. em. Gouan (**BT**)
Paeonia officinalis L. (**HLH**)

Family: Paeoniaceae

Colour: red, purple, pink
Distribution: Alps,
Apennines, Asia Minor,
Armenia
Frequency: rare
Properties: (*flowers and
petals*) antispasmodic,
sedative, narcotic; (*seeds*)
emetic cathartic; to be used
with prudence

Sempervivum montanum L., 1753, subsp. *montanum*
Sempervivum montanum L. (**F**) (**BT**) (**HLH**)

Family: Crassulaceae

Colour: dark red, violet red, violet pink, violet purple
Distribution: Alps, Tuscan Apennines, Apuan Alps, Pyrenees, Carpathians, Corsica
Frequency: uncommon (endemic)

Epilobium angustifolium L., 1753
Epilobium angustifolium L. (**F**) (**BT**) (**HLH**)

Family: Onagraceae
Colour: purple red, pink, white
Distribution: Europe, central and northern Asia, North America
Frequency: common

Primula minima L., 1753
Primula minima L. (**F**) (**HLH**)

Family: Primulaceae

Colour: red, purple red, pink
Distribution: eastern Alps, south-east Europe, Sudeten mtns, Carpathians, Balkans, Bulgaria
Frequency: rare (endemic)

Juncus jacquinii L., 1767
Juncus Jacquinii L. (**F**) (**HLH**)

Family: Juncaceae

Colour: brownish red, brownish purple, brownish black
Distribution: Alps, northern Apennines, Carpathians
Frequency: rare

Lilium bulbiferum L., 1753 var. ***croceum*** (Chaix) Pers., 1786
Lilium bulbiferum L. var. *croceum* (Chaix) Fiori (**F**)
Lilium croceum Chaix (**HLH**)

Family: Liliaceae

Colour: red, orange, reddish orange, yellowy orange
Distribution: central and southern Europe
Frequency: rare

Cypripedium calceolus L., 1753
Cypripedium Calceolus L. (**F**) (**HLH**)

Family: Orchidaceae

Colour: (*three tepals*)
brownish red, purplish red,
ochre red; (*labellum*) yellow
Distribution: Alps,
northern Apennines,
Europe, Caucasus, Siberia,
Korea, China
Frequency: very rare
Properties: (*rhizome*)
antispasmodic, neurotonic,
anticolitic

Silene vallesia L., 1759, subsp. ***vallesia***

Silene vallesia L. var. *typica* (**F**)
Silene vallesia L. (**BT**) (**HLH**)

Family: Caryophyllaceae

Colour: pink
Distribution: Alps, Apuan Alps, central Apennines
Frequency: rare

Silene acaulis (L.) Jacq., 1762
Silene acaulis L. var. *vulgaris* Reichenb. (**F**)
Silene acaulis (L.) Jacq. (**BT**) (**HLH**)

Family: Caryophyllaceae

Colour: pink, purplish red
Distribution: Alps, central and Tuscan Apennines, arctic Europe, Iceland, Pyrenees, Carpathians, Asia, Greenland, North America
Frequency: common

Saponaria ocymoides L., 1753
Saponaria ocymoides L. var. *tipica* (**F**)
Saponaria ocymoides L. (**BT**) (**HLH**)

Family: Caryophyllaceae

Colour: pink, red, purple
Distribution: southern Europe, Asia Minor
Frequency: common
Properties: (*leaves*) *external use:* anti-eruptive and fluidizing, disinfectant; poisonous in large doses

Dianthus superbus L., 1755
Dianthus superbus L. var. *typicus* (**F**)
Dianthus superbus L. (**BT**) (**HLH**)

Family: Caryophyllaceae

Colour: pink, purplish pink, violet pink, purplish violet
Distribution: Alps, northern Apennines, Europe, Siberia, central Asia
Frequency: very rare
Properties: (*petals*) sudorific, diuretic

Thalictrum aquilegifolium L., 1753
Thalictrum aquilegifolium L. (**F**) (**BT**) (**HLH**)

Family: Ranunculaceae

Colour: pink, pale lilac, white

Distribution: Alps, Apennines, Europe, northern Russia, Asia (from the Altais to Japan)

Frequency: common

Petrocallis pyrenaica (L.) R. Br. in Aiton

Petrocallis pyrenaica R. Br. (**F**)
Petrocallis pyrenaica (L.) R. Br. (**BT**) (**HLH**)
Draba pyrenaica L. (*)

Family: Cruciferae

Colour: violet pink, lilac, white
Distribution: Alps, Pyrenees, Carpathians
Frequency: rare (endemic)

Rhodiola rosea L., 1753

Sedum roseum Scop. (**F**)
Sedum Rosea (L.) Scop. (**BT**) (**HLH**)
Sedum Rhodiola DC. (*)

Family: Crassulaceae

Colour: pink, yellowish
pink, yellow
Distribution: Alps,
northern (Paduan)
Apennines, Europe, central
and northern Asia, Japan,
North America
Frequency: rare

Rosa vosagiaca Desportes, 1828

Rosa glauca Vill. var. *typica* (**F**)
Rosa vosagiaca Desp. (**BT**) (**HLH**)
Rosa afzeliana Fries subsp. *vosagiaca* (Desp.) R. Keller & Gams (*)

Rosa glauca Pourret subsp. *reuteri* (Godet) Hayek (*)

Family: Rosaceae

Colour: bright pink, pink
Distribution: Alps, Apennines, Europe (not Iceland), north-east Africa, Asia, North America
Frequency: uncommon
Properties: (*leaves*) astringent; (*petals*) laxative, refreshing; (*fruits*) astringent, corrective, vitaminic; used for jams and liqueurs

Ononis repens L., 1753

Ononis spinosa L. var. *foetens* (All.) (ex Chiov.) Fiori (**F**)
Ononis repens L. (**BT**) (**HLH**)
Ononis procurrens Wallr. (*****)
Ononis spinosa L. subsp. *procurrens* (Wallr.) Briq. (*****)

Family: Leguminosae

Colour: pink, purple
Distribution: Alps, Europe, Macedonia, Morocco
Frequency: common
Properties: (*roots*) depurative, antirheumatic; (*leaves*) diuretic, depurative

Daphne cneorum L., 1753

Daphne Cneorum L. var. *typica* (**F**)
Daphne Cneorum L. (**BT**) (**HLH**)

Family: Thymelaeaceae

Colour: pink, bright pink, red
Distribution: Alps, northern and central Apennines, central Europe, Bulgaria, Ukraine
Frequency: uncommon (endemic)
Properties: (*fruit*) drastic purgative

Erica herbacea L., 1753
Erica carnea L. (**F**) (**BT**) (**HLH**)

Family: Ericaceae

Colour: pink, violet pink, red, dark red, purple
Distribution: Alps, high Apennines, central and southern Europe, Balkans, Carpathians
Frequency: common (endemic)
Properties: (*leaves, flowering tips*) sudorific, diuretic, galattogogue

Rhododendron hirsutum L., 1753
Rhododendron hirsutum L. (**F**) (**BT**) (**HLH**)

Family: Ericaceae

Colour: pink, deep pink
Distribution: Alps, northern Yugoslavia
Frequency: uncommon (endemic)
Properties: (*leaves*) antirheumatic, antilithiasic; to be used with caution

Loiseleuria procumbens (L.) Desv., 1813

Azalea procumbens L. (**F**)
Loiseleuria procumbens (L.) Desv. (**BT**) (**HLH**)

Family: Ericaceae

Colour: pink, red, pale pink
Distribution: Alps, Pyrenees, Britain, Lapland, Iceland, Carpathians, Asia (from the Altais to Japan), arctic America, Greenland
Frequency: common
Properties: (*leaves*) diaphoretic, diuretic; to be used with caution

Primula farinosa L., 1753, subsp. ***farinosa***

Primula farinosa L. var. *typica* (**F**)
Primula farinosa L. (**BT**) (**HLH**)

Family: Primulaceae

Colour: pink, lilac pink, pale purple, dark purple, reddish lilac

Distribution: Alps, mountainous and arctic regions of Europe, Asia, North and South America (Andes)

Frequency: common

Androsace alpina (L.) Lam., 1778

Androsace alpina Lam. var. *typica* (**F**)
Androsace alpina (L.) Lam. (**BT**) (**HLH**)
Androsace glacialis Hoppe (*)

Family: Primulaceae

Colour: pink, pale pink, white, deep pink, reddish pink, red
Distribution: Alps
Frequency: uncommon (endemic)

Armeria maritima (Miller) Willd., 1809
subsp. **alpina** (Willd.) P. Silva, 1971

Armeria vulgaris W. var. *alpina* (W.) Fiori (**F**)
Armeria alpina (DC.) Willd. (**BT**) (**HLH**)
Satice montana Miller (*)

Family: Plumbaginaceae

Colour: pink, purple, red, lilac pink
Distribution: Alps, Pyrenees, Carpathians, Balkans
Frequency: rare (endemic)
Properties: (*leaves and aerial parts*) astringent

Veronica urticifolia Jacq., 1773

Veronica urticoefolia Jacq. (**F**)
Veronica latifolia L. em. Scop. (**BT**)
Veronica latifolia L. (**HLH**)

Family:
Scrophulariaceae

Colour: pink, lilac, white, blue
Distribution: Alps, Apuan Alps, Apennines, Pyrenees, Balkans, Carpathians, Urals
Frequency: common (endemic)
Properties: (*flowering tips*) tonic stomachic

Petasites paradoxus (Retz.) Baumg., 1816

Petasites paradoxus Baumg. var. *typicus* (**F**)
Petasites paradoxus (Retz.) Baumg. (**BT**) (**HLH**)
Petasites niveus (Vill.) Baumg. (*****)

Family: Compositae

Colour: pink, pale pink
Distribution: Alps,
Pyrenees, Jura, Carpathians,
Balkans
Frequency: rare (endemic)

Centaurea scabiosa L., 1753
Centaurea Scabiosa L. var. *calcarea* (Jord.) Fiori (**F**)
Centaurea Scabiosa L. (**BT**) (**HLH**)

Family: Compositae

Colour: pink, reddish pink, purple
Distribution: Valle d'Aosta, Maritime Alps, central Alps, France
Frequency: uncommon
Properties: (*roots*) bitter stomachic, carminative, antithermic

Bulbocodium vernum L., 1753

Bulbocodium vernum L. (**F**)
Colchicum Bulbocodium Ker-Gawl. (**HLH**)

Family: Liliaceae

Colour: pink, lilac pink, lilac
Distribution: Piedmontese and Maritime Alps, Pyrenees, Serbia, southern Russia, Caucasus
Frequency: rare

Gymnadenia conopsea (L.) R. Br. in Aiton, 1813
Gymnadenia conopsea R. Br. var. *typica* (**F**)
Gymnadenia conopsea (L.) R. Br. (**HLH**)

Family: Orchidaceae

Colour: pink, purplish
pink, violet pink, reddish
violet, lilac, violet
Distribution: Apennines,
Britain, Europe, Caucasus,
Asia Minor, northern Iran,
Asia, Siberia, northern
China, Korea, Japan,
Manchuria
Frequency: common
Properties: (*plant*) anti-
epileptic; (*tubers*) emollient,
antispasmodic

Hepatica nobilis Miller, 1768

Anemone Hepatica L. var. *macrantha* Goir. (**F**)
Hepatica nobilis Schreber (**BT**)
Hepatica triloba Gilib. (**HLH**)

Family: Ranunculaceae

Colour: violet, blue, pink, white
Distribution: Europe, Siberia, Japan, North America
Frequency: common

Pulsatilla montana (Hoppe) Reichenb., 1832

Anemone Pulsatilla L. var. *montana* (Hpe.) Fiori (**F**)
Pulsatilla montana (Hoppe) Reichenb. (**BT**) (**HLH**)
Anemone montana Hoppe (*)

Family: Ranunculaceae

Colour: dark violet, dark bluish violet
Distribution: Alps, Carpathians, Balkans
Frequency: rare (endemic)
Properties: (*whole plant*) anti-arthritic, sudorific, febrifuge, narcotic, sedative; to be used with caution

Pulsatilla Halleri (All.) Willd., 1809, subsp. ***halleri***

Anemone Pulsatilla L. var. *Halleri* (All.) Fiori (**F**)
Pulsatilla Halleri (All.) Willd. (**BT**) (**HLH**)
Anemone Halleri All. (*)

Family: Ranunculaceae

Colour: violet, pale violet, pinkish violet
Distribution: Piedmontese and Lombard Alps, Carpathians, Balkans, Crimea
Frequency: rare
Properties: (*whole plant*) febrifuge, anticonvulsive, narcotic sedative; to be used with caution

Clematis alpina (L.) Miller, 1768, subsp. ***alpina***

Clematis alpina Mill. (**F**)
Clematis alpina (L.) Miller (**BT**) (**HLH**)
Atragene alpina L. (*)

Family: Ranunculaceae

Colour: violet, bluish violet
Distribution: Alps and
Emilian Apennines, central
and southern Europe,
Carpathians, Balkans
Frequency: uncommon
Properties: (*leaves*)
revulsive, irritant

Oxytropis halleri Bunge ex Koch, 1843, subsp. *halleri*

Astragalus uralensis L. var. *sericeus* (Lam.) Fiori (**F**)
Oxytropis Halleri Bunge (**BT**) (**HLH**)
Oxytropis sericea (DC.) Simonkai, not Nutt. (*)
Astragalus sericeus Lam.
pro parte (*)
Family: Leguminosae

Colour: violet, lilac violet, bluish violet, reddish violet, lilac
Distribution: Alps, Scotland, Pyrenees, Carpathians
Frequency: rare (endemic)

Viola suavis Bieb., 1819

Viola hirta L. var. *Beraudii* (Bor.) Fiori (**F**)
Viola Wolfiana W. Becker (**BT**)
Viola suavis M. Bieb. (**HLH**)
Viola austriaca A. & J. Kerner (*)
Viola Beraudii Boreau (*)
Viola sepincola Jordan (*)
Viola pontica W. Becker (*)

Family: Violaceae

Colour: violet, bluish violet
Distribution: central and southern Europe, Asia Minor, central Russia
Frequency: rare
Properties: (*rhizome*) purgative, emetic; (*flowers*) bechic, diaphoretic, emollient

Viola calcarata L., 1753
Viola calcarata L. var. *typica* (**F**)
Viola calcarata L. (**BT**) (**HLH**)

Family: Violaceae

Colour: violet, purple, pink
(also yellow and very
occasionally white)
Distribution: Alps,
Balkans
Frequency: common
Properties: (*root*) irritant,
vomitory; (*flowers*) bechic,
pectoral, diaphoretic,
emollient, laxative (light)

Gentianella campestris (L.) Börner, 1912
Gentiana campestris L. (**F**) (**BT**) (**HLH**)
Gentianella campestris (L.) Börner (*)

Family: Gentianaceae

Colour: violet, bluish violet, lilac violet (white)
Distribution: Alps, Apennines (down to Abruzzo), Europe
Frequency: common (endemic)
Properties: (*plant*) bitter, febrifuge; it provides a substance used as a dye or an aromatic

Note: the corolla has four lobes

Gentianella germanica (Willd.) E. F. Warburg in Clapham, Tutin & E. F. Warburg, 1952

Gentiana Amarella L. var. *germanica* (W.) Fiori (**F**)
Gentiana germanica Willd.
(**BT**) (**HLH**)

Family: Gentianaceae

Colour: violet, reddish violet

Distribution: Alps, central and western Europe, Carpathians

Frequency: rare (endemic)

Properties: (*plant*) aperitive, stomachic; it provides an aromatic and colouring substance

Linaria alpina (L.) Miller, 1768
Linaria alpina Mill. (**F**)
Linaria alpina (L.) Miller (**BT**) (**HLH**)

Family:
Scrophulariaceae

Colour: violet, bluish violet
Distribution: Alps, central
Apennines, Pyrenees,
Carpathians, Balkans
Frequency: uncommon
(endemic)

Campanula glomerata L., 1753

Campanula glomerata L. (**F**) (**BT**) (**HLH**)

Family: Campanulaceae

Colour: violet, bluish violet, azure violet, purplish azure, azure

Distribution: central Europe, northern Italy, northern Greece, Asia Minor, central and western Asia, North America (naturalised)

Frequency: common

Campanula spicata L., 1753
Campanula spicata L. (**F**) (**BT**) (**HLH**)

Family: Campanulaceae
Colour: violet, bluish violet, azure violet, azure
Distribution: Alps, Apuan Alps, northern and central Apennines
Frequency: rare (endemic)

Campanula rhomboidalis L., 1753

Campanula rhomboidalis L. var. *typica* (**F**)
Campanula rhomboidalis L. (**BT**) (**HLH**)

Family: Campanulaceae

Colour: violet, azure violet,
azure, blue, bluish violet
Distribution: western and
central Alps, Pyrenees
Frequency: common
(endemic)

Campanula cochlearifolia Lam., 1785

Campanula rotundifolia L. var. *cochlearifolia* (Lam.) Fiori (**F**)
Campanula cochlearifolia Lam. (**BT**) (**HLH**)
Campanula pusilla Haenke (*)

Family: Campanulaceae

Colour: violet, blue, bluish lilac, azure, lilac, white
Distribution: Alps, northern and central Apennines, Pyrenees, Carpathians, Balkans
Frequency: common (endemic)

Phyteuma ovatum Honckeny, 1782

Phyteuma Halleri All. var. *typicum* (**F**)
Phyteuma ovatum Honckeny (**BT**) (**HLH**)
Phyteuma Halleri All. (*)

Family: Campanulaceae

Colour: violet, blackish violet, bluish black
Distribution: Alps, northern Apennines, Pyrenees, Balkans
Frequency: common (endemic)

Aster alpinus L., 1753

Aster alpinus L. var. *typicus* (**F**)
Aster alpinus L. (**BT**) (**HLH**)

Family: Compositae

Colour: violet, bluish violet, lilac, azure violet, pink, white

Distribution: Alps, northern and central Apennines, Europe, Carpathians, Balkans, Urals, northern Russia, Caucasus, Siberia, Armenia, Iran, central Asia, Kamchatka, North America

Frequency: common

Muscari comosum (L.) Miller, 1768

Muscari comosum Mill. var. *typicum* (**F**)
Muscari comosum (L.) Miller (**HLH**)
Leopoldia comosa (L.) Parl. (*)

Family: Liliaceae

Colour: violet, azure violet
Distribution: central and
southern Europe, western
Asia, northern Africa
Frequency: very common
Properties: (*bulbs*)
emollient, astringent (light)

Iris latifolia (Miller) Voss in Siebert et Voss, 1895
Iris xiphioides Ehrh. (*)

Family: Iridaceae

Colour: bright blue
Distribution: Pyrenees,
Spanish Cordillera
Frequency: rare (endemic)

Larix decidua Miller, 1768
Larix decidua Miller (**F**) (**BT**) (**HLH**)

Family: Pinaceae

Colour: purplish red, violet
red
Distribution: Alps,
Carpathians
Frequency: very common
Properties: (*resin*)
anticatarrhal, diuretic,
haemostatic

Note : a tree growing to a height of
52m (170ft); it is the only European
conifer to shed its leaves in winter; the
female flowers are red, the male ones
brown; used for its wood and the
extraction of oil of turpentine

Dianthus glacialis Haenke in Jacq., 1789
Dianthus glacialis Haenke (**F**) (**BT**) (**HLH**)

Family: Caryophyllaceae

Colour: purple, pink, bright pink
Distribution: eastern Alps, Carpathians
Frequency: rare (endemic)

Corydalis solida (L.) Swartz, 1817
Corydalis solida Sw. var. *typica* (**F**)
Corydalis solida (Miller) Clairv. (**BT**)
Corydalis solida (L.) Swartz (**HLH**)

Family: Papaveraceae

Colour: purple, dark red, pink, white
Distribution: Alps, Apennines, Europe, western, northern and eastern Asia, Algerian Atlas
Frequency: rare
Properties: (*tubercles*) sedative, narcotic, diaphoretic, depurative; to be used with caution

Thlaspi rotundifolium (L.) Gaudin, 1829, subsp. ***rotundifolium***

Thlaspi rotundifolium Gaud. var. *corymbosum* Gaud. (**F**)
Thlaspi rotundifolium (L.) Gaudin ssp. *corymbosum* (J. Gay) Gremli (**BT**)
Thlaspi corymbosum (Gay) Rchb. (**HLH**)

Family: Cruciferae

Colour: dark lilac, pale
violet, purple, bright pink
Distribution: Val d'Aosta,
Monte Rosa, Mt Cenis,
Savoy, Swiss Alps
Frequency: rare

Saxifraga oppositifolia L.., 1753
Saxifraga oppositifolia L. var. *distans* Ser. (**F**)
Saxifraga oppositifolia L. (**BT**) (**HLH**)

Family: Saxifragaceae

Colour: purple, lilac red, pink

Distribution: western and Maritime Alps, Sierra Nevada, Pyrenees, Carpathians, northern Europe, northern Siberia, North America, Greenland

Frequency: uncommon

Saxifraga retusa Gouan, 1773
subsp. ***augustana*** (Vacc.) D. A. Webb, 1963

Saxifraga retusa Gouan var. *augustana* L. Vacc. (**F**)
Saxifraga retusa Gouan (**BT**)
Saxifraga purpurea All.
(**HLH**)

Family: Saxifragaceae

Colour: purple red, purple
Distribution: western and
Maritime Alps, Savoy
Frequency: rare

Astragalus danicus Retz., 1783

Astragalus Hypoglottis L. var. *danicus* (Retz.) Fiori (**F**)
Astragalus danicus Retz. (**HLH**)
Astragalus hypoglottis auct.? not L. (*)

Family: Leguminosae

Colour: purple, bluish purple, bluish violet, violet
Distribution: Maritime and Piedmontese Alps, Ireland, central Europe, Caucasus, Siberia, central Asia, North America
Frequency: rare

Astragalus monspessulanus L., 1753

Astragalus monspessulanus L. var. *typicus* (**F**)
Astragalus monspessulanus L. (**BT**) (**HLH**)

Family: Leguminosae

Colour: bright purple,
reddish purple, violet purple
Distribution: southern
Europe to Sicily, Balkans,
Rumania, north-west Africa
(Tunisia, Algeria)
Frequency: common

Trifolium alpinum L., 1753
Trifolium alpinum L. (**F**) (**BT**) (**HLH**)

Family: Leguminosae

Colour: purple, reddish purple, pink
Distribution: Alps, Apuan Alps, Ligurian Apennines, Tuscan and central Apennines, Pyrenees
Frequency: common (endemic)

Epilobium fleischeri Hochst., 1826

Epilobium Dodonaci Vill. var. *alpinum* Burn (**F**)
Epilobium fleischeri Hochst. (**BT**) (**HLH**)

Family: Onagraceae

Colour: purple, bright pink
Distribution: Alps
Frequency: common

Soldanella alpina L., 1753

Soldanella alpina L. var. *typica* (**F**)
Soldanella alpina L. (**BT**) (**HLH**)

Family: Primulaceae

Colour: lilac, azure violet, bluish violet, blue, violet
Distribution: Alps, Apennines, Pyrenees
Frequency: common (endemic)
Properties: (*roots*) purgative

Gentiana purpurea L., 1753
Gentiana purpurea L. var. *typica* (**F**)
Gentiana purpurea L. (**BT**) (**HLH**)

Family: Gentianaceae

Colour: purple, reddish purple

Distribution: western and central Alps, northern Apennines, Apuan Alps, Scandinavia, Carpathians, Caucasus, Kamchatka

Frequency: rare (endemic)

Properties: (*roots*) antifermentative, aperitive, bitter tonic, digestive, febrifuge, vermifuge; its tincture is used to treat digestive troubles

Scutellaria alpina L., 1753, subsp. *alpina*

Family: Labiatae

Colour: purple, azure violet, bluish violet, violet
Distribution: Alps, northern and central Apennines, Pyrenees, Balkans, central Asia, Siberia, Altais, Urals, Turkestan, Ukraine
Frequency: rare

Pedicularis verticillata L., 1753
Pedicularis verticillata L. (**F**) (**BT**) (**HLH**)

Family:
Scrophulariaceae

Colour: purple, reddish
purple, violet purple, pink
Distribution: Alps, Apuan
Alps, northern and central
Apennines, Europe,
northern and central Asia,
North America
Frequency: common

Carduus defloratus L., 1759
Carduus defloratus L. (**F**) (**BT**) (**HLH**)

Family: Compositae

Colour: purple, red, pink
Distribution: Alps, Apennines, central Europe, Carpathians
Frequency: common

Cirsium eriophorum (L.) Scop., 1772

Cirsium eriophorum Scop. (**F**)
Cirsium eriophorum (L.) Scop. (**BT**) (**HLH**)

Family: Compositae

Colour: purple, lilac, reddish purple
Distribution: western Alps, Apennines
Frequency: common

Centaurea uniflora Turra, 1765
subsp. ***nervosa*** (Willd.) Bonnier & Layens, 1894

Centaurea uniflora Turra var. *nervosa* (W.) Fiori (**F**)
Centaurea nervosa Willd. (**BT**) (**HLH**)
Centaurea uniflora Turra
ssp. *nervosa* Rouy (*)

Family: Compositae

Colour: purple, violet, reddish purple
Distribution: Alps, northern Apennines, Balkans, Carpathians
Frequency: rare (endemic)

Allium schoenoprasum L., 1753

Allium Schoenoprasum L. var. *sibiricum* (L.) Fiori (**F**)
Allium Schoenoprasum L. (**HLH**)

Family: Liliaceae

Colour: lilac, pink, pinkish purple, violet purple, pinkish violet, bluish pink, azure violet

Distribution: Alps, central and southern Europe, Siberia, Himalayas, Japan, North America

Frequency: common

Properties: (*bulb*) stimulant, digestive, carminative, antiseptic, powerful intestinal microbicide, balsamic, diuretic, antinicotinic, vermifuge

Lilium martagon L., 1753
Lilium Martagon L. var. *typicum* (**F**)
Lilium Martagon L. (**HLH**)

Family: Liliaceae

Colour: purple, pink, purplish pink, purplish red, white
Distribution: Alps, Apennines, central and southern Europe, Caucasus, Asia to Japan
Frequency: common
Properties: (*bulb*) diuretic, antiarthritic; *external use:* emollient, resolutive

Orchis mascula (L.) L., 1755
Orchis mascula L. (**F**) (**HLH**)

Family: Orchidaceae

Colour: purple, purplish red, pink, red, lilac
Distribution: Sardinia, central and southern Europe, central Russia, Asia Minor, Caucasus, Iran, Urals, northern Africa (Morocco, Algeria)
Frequency: common
Properties: (*tuber*) emollient, excipient

Orchis incarnata L., 1755

Orchis latifolia L. var. *incarnata* (L.) Fiori (**F**)
Orchis incarnata L. (**HLH**)
Orchis latifolia L. sec. Pugsl. (*)
Dactylorhiza incarnata (L.)
Soó, 1962

Family: Orchidaceae

Colour: purple, pink,
carmine red, violet pink
Distribution: central and
southern Europe, Siberia,
central Asia, Mongolia
Frequency: uncommon
Properties: (*tuber*)
emollient, excipient

Nigritella nigra (L.) Reichenb. fil., 1851

Nigritella nigra Rchb. (**F**)
Nigritella nigra (L.) Rchb. (**HLH**)
Nigritella angustifolia Rich. (*****)

Family: Orchidaceae

Colour: purple, purplish
black, reddish black, reddish
brown, red, pink
Distribution: Alps,
Apennines, Pyrenees, Jura,
Carpathians, Balkans,
Scandinavia
Properties: (*aerial parts*)
aphrodisiac

Note: vanilla-scented flowers

Gentiana acaulis L., 1753

Gentiana acaulis L. var. *latifolia* Gr. & Godr. (**F**)
Gentiana Kochiana Perr. & Song. (**BT**) (**HLH**)
Gentiana excisa C. Presl. (*)

Family: Gentianaceae

Colour: blue, dark azure, dark blue
Distribution: Alps, Apuan Alps, northern and central Apennines, Pyrenees, Balkans, Carpathians
Frequency: common (endemic)
Properties: (*whole plant*) bitter aperitive, tonic, stomachic, febrifuge

Gentiana verna L., 1753
Gentiana verna L. (**F**) (**BT**) (**HLH**)

Family: Gentianaceae
Colour: dark azure, violet, blue, dark blue
Distribution: Alps, Apennines, Ireland, England, Pyrenees, Balkans, Carpathians, Asia Minor, Caucasus, Turkestan, Afghanistan, Altais, eastern Siberia, Mongolia
Frequency: common
Properties: bitter aperitive

Gentiana brachyphylla Vill., 1779
Gentiana verna L. var. *brachyphylla* (Vill.) Fiori (**F**)
Gentiana brachyphylla Vill. (**BT**) (**HLH**)

Family: Gentianaceae

Colour: azure, dark azure, pale blue, blue
Distribution: Alps, Sierra Nevada, Pyrenees
Frequency: rare
Properties: bitter aperitive

Gentiana bavarica L., 1753
Gentiana bavarica L. var. *typica* (**F**)
Gentiana bavarica L. (**BT**) (**HLH**)

Family: Gentianaceae

Colour: azure, dark blue, violet
Distribution: Alps
Frequency: uncommon (endemic)
Properties: bitter aperitive

Echium vulgare L., 1753

Echium vulgare L. var. *typicum* (**F**)
Echium vulgare L. (**BT**) (**HLH**)

Family: Boraginaceae

Colour: blue, violet blue, violet, pink
Distribution: Europe, western Asia, western Siberia, northern Africa, North America (naturalised)
Frequency: very common
Properties: (*flowering spike*) sudorific, pectoral, anti-inflammatory, anticatarrhal

Veronica chamaedrys L., 1753

Veronica Chamaedrys L. var. *typica* (**F**)
Veronica Chamaedrys L. (**BT**) (**HLH**)

Family:
Scrophulariaceae

Colour: blue, azure blue, azure, pink
Distribution: Europe, Asia Minor, Siberia, Caucasus, central Asia, North America
Frequency: very common
Properties: (*flowering tips*) tonic, stomachic, bechic, astringent

Phyteuma hemisphericum L., 1753
Phyteuma hemisphericum L. var. *graminifolium* (Sieb.) Fiori (**F**)
Phyteuma hemisphericum L. (**BT**) (**HLH**)

Family: Campanulaceae

Colour: blue, bluish violet
Distribution: Alps,
Apennines, Pyrenees
Frequency: common
(endemic)

Scilla bifolia L., 1753
Scilla bifolia L. var. *typica* (**F**)
Scilla bifolia L. (**HLH**)

Family: Liliaceae

Colour: blue, azure, bluish azure, purplish blue, white, bluish pink, pink
Distribution: central and southern Europe, Sicily and Sardinia, Asia Minor, Caucasus
Frequency: uncommon
Properties: (*bulb*) cardiotonic, diuretic, expectorant

Aquilegia alpina L., 1753

Aquilegia alpina L. var. *typica* (**F**)
Aquilegia alpina L. (**BT**) (**HLH**)

Family: Ranunculaceae

Colour: azure, violet azure, blue
Distribution: Piedmontese Alps, Tuscan Apennines
Frequency: rare (endemic)

Linum perenne L., 1753, subsp. ***alpinum*** (Jacq.) Ockendon, 1967

Linum perenne L. var. *alpinum* (Jacq.) Fiori (**F**)
Linum alpinum Jacq. (**BT**) (**HLH**)

Family: Geraniaceae

Colour: azure
Distribution: Alps, Apennines, central and southern Europe, northern Urals
Frequency: rare
Properties: (*whole plant*) equine purgative

Gentiana clusii Perr. et Song 1855
Gentiana acaulis L. var. *vulgaris* Neilr. (**F**)
Gentiana clusii Perr. & Song (**BT**) (**HLH**)

Family: Gentianaceae

Colour: azure, intense azure
Distribution: rare (endemic)
Properties: (*whole plant with leaves*) bitter aperitive, tonic, stomachic, febrifuge

Gentianella ciliata (L.) Borkh. 1796
Gentiana ciliata L. var. *typica* (**F**)
Gentiana ciliata L. (**BT**) (**HLH**)

Family: Gentianaceae

Colour: azure, pale blue, blue
Distribution: Alps, northern and central Apennines, Pyrenees, Balkans, Carpathians, Ukraine, Caucasus
Frequency: rare

Myosotis alpestris F. W. Schmidt, 1794

Myosotis alpestris Schm. var. *typica* (**F**)
Myosotis alpestris F. W. Schmidt (**BT**) (**HLH**)
Myosotis pyrenaica Auct. (*)
Myosotis sylvatica Hoffm.
subsp. *alpestris* (F. W.
Schmidt) Gams (*)

Family: Boraginaceae

Colour: azure, dark azure,
blue
Distribution: Alps,
Apennines, Pyrenees,
Balkans
Frequency: common
Properties: (*aerial parts*)
slightly astringent

Eritrichium nanum (L.) Schrader ex Gaudin, 1828, subsp. ***nanum***

Eritrichium nanum Schrad. (**F**)
Eritrichium nanum (L.) Gaud. (**BT**)
Eritrichium nanum (Amann) Schrader (**HLH**)
Myosotis nana Amann (*)

Family: Boraginaceae

Colour: azure
Distribution: Alps, Carpathians
Frequency: rare

Ajuga pyramidalis L., 1753
Ajuga genevensis L. var. *pyramidalis* (L.) Fiori (**F**)
Ajuga pyramidalis L. (**BT**) (**HLH**)

Family: Labiatae

Colour: azure, violet azure, violet blue, pink
Distribution: Alps, Ligurian Apennines, Europe, Caucasus
Frequency: common

Veronica fruticans Jacq., 1762

Veronica fruticulosa L. var. *fruticans* (Jacq.) Fiori (**F**)
Veronica fruticans Jacq. (**BT**) (**HLH**)
Veronica saxatilis Scop. (*)

Family:
Scrophulariaceae

Colour: azure, blue
Distribution: Alps, Apuan
Alps, northern and central
Apennines, Europe,
Carpathians, Balkans
Frequency: common

Globularia cordifolia L., 1753
Globularia cordifolia L. (**F**) (**BT**) (**HLH**)

Family: Globulariaceae

Colour: azure, azure grey, azure pink, blue, white
Distribution: Alps, Apuan Alps, central and southern Apennines, Balkans, Carpathians, Crimea
Frequency: common (endemic)

Note: single flowers, irregularly bellshaped

Globularia nudicaulis L., 1753
Globularia nudicaulis L. (**F**) (**BT**) (**HLH**)

Family: Globulariaceae

Colour: azure, blue
Distribution: Alps,
northern Apennines,
Pyrenees
Frequency: common
Properties: (*leaves*)
diuretic, bitter tonic,
stomachic, light purgative,
diaphoretic

Note: single flower; irregular
bellshaped corolla

Campanula cenisia L., 1763
Campanula cenisisa L. (**F**) (**BT**) (**HLH**)

Family: Campanulaceae

Colour: azure, blue, azure
lilac
Distribution: Valtellina,
Piedmont, Ticinese Alps
Frequency: very rare
(endemic)

Campanula barbata L., 1759

Campanula barbata L. var. *typica* (**F**)
Campanula barbata L. (**BT**) (**HLH**)

Family: Campanulaceae

Colour: azure, pale azure, bluish lilac, blue, white
Distribution: Alps, central and southern Europe, Norway, Sudeten mtns, western Carpathians
Frequency: common (endemic)

Centaurea triumfetti All., 1773

Centaurea montana L. var. *Triumfetti* (All.) Fiori (**F**)
Centaurea Triumfetti All. (**BT**)
Centaurea Triumfettii All. (**HLH**)
Centaurea axillaris Willd.
(*)
Centaurea lugdunensis
Gaudin (*)

Family: Compositae

Colour: azure, blue, violet, purplish red
Distribution: Alps, Apennines, Pyrenees, Carpathians, Balkans, Asia Minor, Caucasus, northern Africa (Morocco)
Frequency: common

Equisetum sylvaticum L., 1753
Equisetum sylvaticum L. (**F**) (**BT**) (**HLH**)

Family: Equisetaceae

Colour: green
Distribution: Alps, northern and central Europe, northern Asia, North America
Frequency: common

Note: Cryptogamous (flowerless) plant, carrying the spores on its strobili

Botrychium lunaria (L.) Schwartz in Schrader, 1802

Botrychium lunaria Sw. var. *typicum* (**F**)
Botrychium lunaria (L.) Sw. (**BT**) (**HLH**)

Family: Ophioglossaceae

Colour: green
Distribution: Europe, northern Asia, Japan, North America, Patagonia, Chile, Australia
Frequency: uncommon
Properties: (*whole plant*) cicatrizing, used to treat sluggish wounds and cancerous sores

Note: Cryptogamous (flowerless) plant carrying its spores on the bunch of spikes

Pinus uncinata Miller ex Mirbel in Buffon, 1806

Pinus Mugo Turra var. *uncinata* (Ram.) Fiori (**F**)
Pinus Mugo Turra ssp. *uncinata* Domin (**HLH**)

Family: Pinaceae

Colour: green, yellowish
green
Distribution: western
Alps, Piedmontese
Apennines, Pyrenees
Frequency: rare
Properties: (*young branches*)
balsamic, anticatarrhal,
antiputrefacient

Juniperus communis L., 1753, subsp. ***communis***
Juniperus communis L. var. *typica* (**F**)
Juniperus communis L. (**BT**) (**HLH**)

Family: Cupressaceae

Colour: green, yellowish green

Distribution: Europe, Algeria, northern and western Asia to the Himalayas, North America

Frequency: common

Properties: (*leaves*) diuretic, anti-eczematous; (*fruits*) aromatic, tonic digestive, sudorific, antigout, antirheumatic, diuretic, disinfectant of the urinary ducts; used in the production of gin

Salix herbacea L., 1753
Salix herbacea L. (**F**) (**BT**) (**HLH**)

Family: Salicaceae

Colour: green, yellowish green

Distribution: Alps, central Apennines, Pyrenees, Carpathians, Balkans, Scotland, Greenland, North America

Frequency: common

Oxyria digyna (L.) Hill, 1768
Oxyria digyna Hill (**F**)
Oxyria digyna (L.) Hill (**BT**) (**HLH**)

Family: Polygonaceae

Colour: grassy green
Distribution: Alps, arctic Europe, Spain, Corsica, Bulgaria
Frequency: common

Chenopodium bonus-henricus L., 1753
Chenopodium Bonus-Henricus L. (**F**) (**BT**) (**HLH**)

Family: Chenopodiaceae

Colour: green, brownish green

Distribution: Alps, Apennines, Sicily, Sardinia, high grounds in central and southern Europe, central Asia, Siberia, China, North America

Frequency: common

Properties: (*whole plant*) antihaemorrhoidal, anti-inflammatory; (*seeds*) laxative

Note: can be cooked like spinach

Minuartia sedoides (L.) Hiern, 1899

Alsine sedoides Kitt. (**F**)
Minuartia sedoides (L.) Hiern (**BT**) (**HLH**)
Cherleria sedoides L. (*****)

Family: Caryophyllaceae

Colour: greenish yellow
Distribution: Alps,
Pyrenees, Carpathians,
Scotland
Frequency: common

Thalictrum minus L., 1753 subsp. ***minus***

Thalictrum foetidum L. var. *minus* (L.) Fiori (**F**)
Thalictrum minus L. (**BT**) (**HLH**)

Family: Ranunculaceae

Colour: greenish, yellowish
Distribution: Alps,
Apennines, Europe,
northern Asia, Ethiopia,
South Africa
Frequency: common

Alchemilla xanthochlora Rothm., 1937

Alchemilla vulgaris L. var. *pratensis* (Schmidt) Fiori (**F**)
Alchemilla vulgaris L. s.l.ssp. *pratensis* (F. W. Schmidt) Camus (**BT**)
Alchemilla xanthochlora Rothm. (**HLH**)
Alchemilla pratensis auct. (*)
Alchemilla sylvestris auct. (*)

Family: Rosaceae

Colour: green, yellowish green, pale green
Distribution: Alps, central Apennines (Pistoia), Europe, western Asia, Siberia, North America
Frequency: very common
Properties: (*leaves*) astringent, diuretic, soothing, sedative; *external use* haemostatic detergent

Euphorbia dulcis L., 1753

Euphorbia dulcis L. var. *typica* (**F**)
Euphorbia dulcis L. (**BT**) (**HLH**)

Family: Euphorbiaceae

Colour: green, yellowish green, then reddish
Distribution: central and western Europe, Macedonia, Ukraine
Frequency: very common (endemic)

Rhamnus pumilus Turra, 1764

Rhamnus pumila Turra var. *typica* (**F**)
Rhamnus pumila Turra (**BT**) (**HLH**)

Family: Rhamnaceae

Colour: green, yellowish green

Distribution: Alps, central and southern Apennines, Sardinia, southern Europe (from Spain to Albania), north-west Africa (Atlas)

Frequency: uncommon (endemic)

Sambucus racemosa L., 1753
Sambucus racemosa L. (**F**) (**BT**) (**HLH**)

Family: Caprifoliaceae

Colour: green, yellowish green

Distribution: Alps, northern Apennines, central Europe, Baltic, Carpathians, Bulgaria

Frequency: very common

Properties: (*bark*) purgative; (*flowers*) sudorific, diuretic, emollient, resolutive; (*fruits*) laxative; berries are used in jam-making

Artemisia genipi Weber in Stechm., 1775

Artemisia Genipi Weber var. _typica_ (**F**)
Artemisia Genipi Weber (**BT**) (**HLH**)
Artemisia spicata Wulfen (*)

Family: Compositae

Colour: green, silvery grey, yellow, brown
Distribution: Alps, Pyrenees
Frequency: rare
Properties: (_flowering parts_) bitter, stimulant, stomachic, digestive, fortifying, excitant, tonic, sudorific, febrifuge, balsamic expectorant, antiscorbutic; used in liqueurs and sweets

Phleum phleoides (L.) Karsten, 1881
Phleum phleoides Simonk., 1886, var. *typicum* (**F**)
Phleum Boehmeri Wibel (**HLH**)

Family: Graminaceae

Colour: green
Distribution: Alps,
Apennines, Mt Etna,
Europe, northern, western
and central Asia, northern
Africa (Algeria)
Frequency: uncommon

Veratrum album L., 1753

Veratrum album L., var. *Lobelianum* (Bernh.) Fiori (**F**)
Veratrum Lobelianum Bernh. (**HLH**)

Family: Liliaceae

Colour: green, pale green, yellowish green
Distribution: Alps, Apennines, Pyrenees, Carpathians, central Asia, Siberia, Kamchatka, Altais, Japan, Arctic
Frequency: common
Properties: (*rhizome*) purgative and vomitory (poisonings), antithermic, depressive of the bulbar centres; (*whole plant*) antidiarrhoeic. *Not for family use.* It is a poisonous plant which is sometimes mistaken for *Gentiana lutea* which is not poisonous

Coeloglossum viride (L.) Hartman, 1820
Coeloglossum viride Hartm. (**F**)
Coeloglossum viride (L.) Hartman (**HLH**)

Family: Orchidaceae

Colour: green, yellowish green

Distribution: Alps, Apennines, Europe, Russia, Urals, Siberia, Crimea, Caucasus, Turkestan, eastern Asia, North America

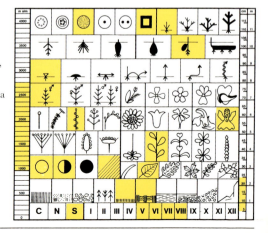

GLOSSARY OF PHARMACEUTICAL TERMINOLOGY

Antidiarrhoetic: controls and moderates intestinal movements.

Anti-eruptive: controls and eliminates the exodus through the mouth of gases which form in the stomach during digestion.

Antihaemorrhagic: controls and stops haemorrhages and blood loss.

Antihelmintic: see Vermifuge.

Antipyretic: see Febrifuge.

Antiscropholous: treats and prevents the swelling and suppuration of lymphatic glands.

Antiseptic: a remedy against putrefaction and germ infections.

Antispasmodic: a sedative of the nervous system: controls muscular contractions.

Antithermic: see Febrifuge.

Aperitive: stimulates the appetite.

Aphrodisiac: a substance which increases sexual stimulus and response.

Aromatic: slightly excitant.

Astringent: contracts tissues, making them more taut, and controls mucous secretions.

Balsamic: controls and reduces strong secretions by soothing the inflamed mucous tissues of the respiratory and urinary ducts.

Bechic: a remedy for coughs and bronchial afflictions.

Bitter: a substance which aids digestion.

Cardiotonic: increases the heart's energy.

Cardiovascular: aids the workings of the circulatory system.

Carminative: diminishes and expels abnormal gases from the digestive system and soothes pain.

Corrective: a substance used to correct the taste and smell of drugs.

Corroborant: a tonic for the whole organism.

Depurative: encourages the expulsion (through sweat or urine) of harmful substances and impurities thus purifying both blood and organism.

Detergent: a substance used to clean wounds and ulcers and encourage cicatrization.

Diaphoretic (sudorific): causes and increases transpiration.

Diuretic: encourages the secretion of urine.

Emetic: provokes vomiting.

Emmenagogue: re-establishes and regulates the menses.

Emollient: soothes and eliminates inflammation of tissues, thus protecting and softening mucous membranes.

Excipient: inert liquid or dough-like substance used to add body to drugs.

Excitant: stimulant.

Expectorant: facilitates the expulsion of bronchial secretions.

Febrifuge: reduces body temperature.

Fluidizer: helps dissolve food in the stomach.

Galactagogue: aids and increases milk secretion.

Haemosolvent: liquefies the blood.

Haemostatic: coagulant, halts haemorrhages.

Hypertensive: lowers the blood pressure.

Insecticide: kills insects.

Irritant: produces inflammation.

Laxative: mild stimulant of intestinal evacuation.

Narcotic: soothing substance which induces sleep.

Neurotonic: tonic for the nervous system.

Pectoral: a drug which treats the tissues affected by ailments of the respiratory ducts.

Purgative: a strong stimulant of intestinal evacuations.

Refreshing: relieves thirst and lowers the temperature of the organism; it also aids the intestinal movements.

Resolutive: a substance which can dispel obstructions, granulomas, inflammations and most ailments in general.

Revulsive: a drug to be used externally; it causes an increase in the blood afflux to the area it is applied to, followed by artificial irritation, which in turn determines the decrease of irritation of the affected internal organ.

Rubefacient: a drug to be used externally; it induces and increases the flow of blood to the surface, causing reddening of the skin.

Sedative: soothes internal and external inflammations.

Stimulant: excites the functions of the nervous, muscular and circulatory systems.

Stomachic: it improves and reinforces the functioning of the stomach.

Sudorific: activates and increases transpiration.

Sympathicolithic: annuls the effect of the sympathetic nervous system.

Tincture: alcoholic infusion of vegetal substances.
Tonic: increases the vitality and energy of the organism.
Topic: a drug applied only and directly to the exterior of the afflicted area.

Vermifuge: destroys and eliminates intestinal worms.
Vomitory: see Emetic.

FURTHER READING

AICHELE, D., *Field Guide to Wild Flowers*, Octopus (1976)

ARY, S. and GREGORY, M., *Oxford Book of Wild Flowers*, OUP (1960)

BACON, L., *Mountain Flower Holidays in Europe*, Alpine Garden Soc (1979)

BAILEY, L. H., *How Plants Get Their Names*, Dover Publications (1933)

BARTLETT, M., *Gentians*, Alpha Books (1975)

BECKETT, K. A. (Ed), *Illustrated Dictionary of Botany*, T. Copplestone (1977)

BINZ, A. and THOMMEN, E., *Flore de la Suisse*, Neuchatel (1966)

BLAMEY, M. and FITTER, R. S. R., *Handguide to the Wild Flowers of Britain and Europe*, Collins (1979)

BLOOM, A., *Alpines For Your Garden*, Floraprint (1980)

BRITTON, N. L. and ROSE, J. N., *Illustrated Flora of the Northern United States and Canada*, Dover Publications (1971)

CHINERY, M., *Guide to Wild Flowers*, Pan (1979)

DAVIS, P. H. and CULLEN, J., *Identification of Flowering Plant Families*, OUP (1979)

EDLIN, H. L., *Atlas of Plant Life*, Heinemann (1973)

ELIOT, ROY, *Alpine Gardening*, Vista Books (1963)

ELLIS, E. A., *Wild Flowers of the Moors and Heaths*, Jarrold (1973)

FIORI, A., *Nuova Flora Analitica d'Italia*, Vols I–III, Basel & Stuttgart (1967–72)

FITTER, ALISTAIR H. (Ed), *Atlas of Wild Flowers of Britain and Northern Europe*, Collins (1978)

FITTER, RICHARD S. R., *Finding Wild Flowers*, Collins (1971)

FITTER, RICHARD S. R. and FITTER, A. H., *Wild Flowers of Britain & Northern Europe*, Collins (1974)

FOSTER, RAYMOND, *Rock Garden & Alpine Plants*, David & Charles (1982)

GILMOUR, J. S. L. and WALTERS, MAX, *Wild Flowers*, Collins (1974)

GOOD, RONALD, *Geography of the Flowering Plants*, Longman (1974)

GRIFFITH, ANNA N., *Alpines & Rock Garden Plants*, Collins (1980)

HAWKSWORTH, D. L., *Changing Flora and Fauna of Britain*, Academic Press (1974)

HEYWOOD, V. H. (Ed), *Flowering Plants of the World*, OUP (1978)

HESS, H. E., LANDOLT, E. and HIRZEL, R., *Flora der Schweiz und angrenzender Gebiete*, Vols I–III, Basel & Stuttgart (1967–72)

HICKEY, M. and KING, C. J., *One Hundred Families of Flowering Plants*, CUP (1981)

HILLS, L. D., *The Propagation of Alpines*, Faber & Faber (1950)

HOLMES, SANDRA, *Flowers of the World*, Bantam Books (1975)

HUXLEY, A., *Mountain Flowers in Colour*, Blandford (1973)

INGWERSEN, WILL, *Manual of Alpine Plants*, Ingwersen & Dunnsprint Ltd (1978)

MARTIN, W. KEEBLE, *Concise British Flora in Colour*, M. Joseph (1975)

MUNZ, P. A. and KECK, D. D., *California Mountain Wild Flowers*, University of California Press (1963)

PERRING, F. H. and WALTERS, MAX (Ed), *Atlas of the British Flora*, (1978)

PERRY, FRANCES, *Flowers of the World*, Hamlyn (1972)

PHILLIPS, R., *Wild Flowers of Britain*, Pan (1978)

PHILLIPSON, W. R. and HEARN, D., *Rock Garden Plants of the Southern Alps*, Caxton Press (1962)

POLUNIN, OLEG, *Flowers of Europe: A Field Guide*, OUP (1969)

POLUNIN, OLEG and WRIGHT, ROBIN S., *Concise Flowers of Europe*, OUP (1972)

ROSE, FRANCIS, *Wild Flower Key*, Warne (1981)

SLAVIK, BONUMIL, *Colour Guide to Familiar Mountain Flowers*, Octopus (1977); *Colour Guide to Familiar Wild Flowers, Ferns and Grasses*, Octopus (1974)

STOKOE, W. J. (Ed), *Observer's Book of Wild Flowers*, Warne (1978)

STURTEVANT, A. H., *Edible Plants of the World*, Dover Publications (1972)

SWINGLEHURST, P. and D'ARBLAY, N., *Plants and Flowers*, Caxton Pub. Co (1974)

TAYLOR, A. W., *Wild Flowers of the Pyrenees*, Chatto (1971)

THOMPSON, H. S., *Alpine Plants of Europe*, Routledge (1911)

TOSCO, UBERTO, *World of Mountain Flowers*, Orbis Publications (1974)

WALTERS, MAX and RAVEN, J., *Mountain Flowers*, New Naturalist, Collins

WIGGINS, I. L. and THOMAS, J. H., *Flora of the Alaskan Arctic Slope*, University of Toronto Press (1961)

WILKIE, D., *Gentians*, Country Life (1936)

WILSON, C. G. and BLAMEY, M., *Alpine Flowers of Britain and Europe*, Collins (1979)

ALPHABETICAL INDEX OF LATIN NAMES

Numbers given refer to colour plates.
Synonyms are in italics

ALPHABETICAL INDEX
OF VERNACULAR NAMES

Numbers given refer to colour plates

WILD HERBS: A FIELD GUIDE
Jacques de Sloover and Martine Goosens

Whether used as a practical identification guide in the field, or for armchair browsing, this book offers a great deal of information succinctly presented. The herbs in the 144 stunning colour plates are grouped by colour. To identify a plant, simply open the guide at the pages bordered by the colour corresponding to that of the flower and you will soon find the plant itself. This ingenious system is time-saving, and the close proximity of illustrations of similarly-coloured flowers helps to avoid misidentification.

For the purposes of this book, a herb is defined as a useful plant, one which is used to cure, to feed, to flavour dishes, to dye wool, or for any other specific aim. Pictograms presented alongside each colour plate summarize other properties—aromatic, medicinal and culinary, which parts are efficacious, when the herb is at its prime, where it grows, when it flowers. This at-a-glance information is supplemented by useful appendices, a glossary and notes on further reading.

210 × 120mm (8¼ × 4¾in) 144 colour plates, 144 pictograms

MUSHROOMS & TOADSTOOLS: A COLOUR FIELD GUIDE
U. Nonis

Anyone interested in collecting mushrooms, whether to study them scientifically or simply to enrich their everyday diet with their nutritional value, will find this book an invaluable guide. It is based on a new descriptive system: each of 168 colour photographs shows specimens in their natural habitat and is accompanied by a pictogram giving identification—at a glance—of their principal characteristics, combining a wealth of information with simplicity of presentation. Identification is further aided by the colours on the margins of the pages which reflect those of the fungi.

An introduction describes the main genera, their habitat, dangerous or valuable properties, and directions for collecting and growing them. Further Reading, Etymology of Scientific Terms and indexes contribute to the unique value of this guide.

210 × 120mm (8¼ × 4¾in) 168 colour plates, 79 line illustrations, 168 pictograms

MINERALS & GEMSTONES: AN IDENTIFICATION GUIDE
Guiseppe Brocardo

A completely new way to approach the mineral world is here offered to the experienced collector and the beginner. The 156 splendid colour photographs are accompanied by a brief description and a pictographic table which provides, through easily recognisable symbols, the available information necessary for identification and classification. The key to the symbols is printed on a bookmark. The margins of the pages are coloured to reflect those of the minerals themselves and aid quick identification.

The colour plates are preceded by extensive information on how to recognise and collect minerals, their origin and formation, their structure and properties, the classification, and how to prepare them for preservation. A glossary, bibliography and indexes complete the volume and add to its values as an indispensable guide for all collectors.

Guiseppe Brocardo was born in 1916 and has a degree in natural sciences. For the past 35 years he has been teaching in Turin, and is director of the Museo di Storia Naturale there. He has personally photographed the museum's collection to illustrate this book, and is a frequent contributor to magazines and periodicals on mineralogy.

210 × 120mm (8¼ × 4¾in) 156 colour plates, 27 line drawings, 156 pictograms

KEY TO SYMBOLS USED

Type of plant

 Plant belonging to the Gymnosperms

 Dicotyledons

 Monocotyledons

Plant cycle

 Annual plant

 Biennial plant

Perennial plant

Kind of plant

 Herbaceous

Sub-shrub

Shrub or bush

Tree

Underground organs
Root

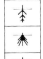 Tap root

Fasciculate roots

Fleshy root

Modified Underground Stem

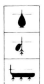 Bulb

Tuber

Rhizome

Stem growth

 Dwarf plant

Cushion-like plant

Spreading plant

 Stoloniferous plant

Erect plant

Rambling plant

Climbing plant

Plant sexuality

 Hermaphrodite

Monoecious plant

Dioecious plant

Inflorescence

 Single flower

Amentum

Spike

Raceme or cluster

Scorpioid cyme

Corymb

Umbel

Flat capitulum

Oblong capitulum

Shape of flowers
Special flowers

 Bare flower

Composite

Flowers with Dialypetalous Corolla

Regular dialypetalous corolla

 Corolla with 4 petals or petaloidal sepals

 Corolla with more than 4 petals, tepals or petaloidal sepals

Irregular diapetalous corolla

Corolla like that of the *Violacae*

Papilionaceous (or similar) corolla

Flowers with Gamopetalous Corolla

Regular gamopetalous corolla

Bell-shaped corolla

Corolla with pronounced petaloidal lobes

Irregular gamopetalous corolla

Corolla with bilateral symmetry, ie divided into 2 parts, labiated or 4-lobed

Corolla with bilateral symmetry, the inferior lobe being different from the others

Position of the leaves on the plant

Rosette

Alternate

Opposed

Verticillate

Imbricated

Shape of leaves

Narrow leaf

Broad leaf

Single leaf with more or less incised margin or lobes

Single leaf indented almost to the centre in the shape of a fan

Composite leaf formed by variously-shaped folioles attached to the same axis

Light requirements

In full sun

In half shade

In full shade

Humidity requirements

Soil humidity

Habitat

Meadows, grasslands

Steppes, stony pastures

Grounds covered in rubble or stones

Woodland

Pastures

Peatbogs and fens

Running or still waters

Gravelly shores and banks

Moraines, screes

Rocks and their fissures

Pedology

C	Basic or alkaline soils, calcareous
N	Neutral soils
S	Acid soils

Phenology

Roman figures: indicating the flowering month

| I | II | III | IV | V | VI | VII | VIII | IX | X | XI | XII |

Altitude limits

Plant height

From 0 to 4,200 m (13,800 ft) above sea level

Scales from 0 to 120 cm (4 ft) and from 0 to 12 m (40 ft)

Plant properties

Poisonous plant

Medicinal plant

Essence-producing plant